*Avalon*
*Abas*

# Nelson Spelling 6

*Maddi.*

**Deb Kekewich and Jim Kekewich**

## Series Authors
Donna Duplak
Deb Kekewich
Jim Kekewich
Clare Kosnik
Louis Quildon
Edgar Schmidt
Catherine Walker
*Clare Kosnik, Senior Author*

I(T)P® Nelson

*an International Thomson Publishing company*

Toronto • Albany • Bonn • Boston • Cincinnati • Detroit • London • Madrid • Melbourne
Mexico City • New York • Pacific Grove • Paris • San Francisco • Singapore • Tokyo • Washington

I(T)P® **International Thomson Publishing**
The ITP logo is a trademark under licence

Published in 1997 by
I(T)P® **Nelson**
A division of Thomson Canada Limited
1120 Birchmount Road
Scarborough, Ontario M1K 5G4

Visit our Website at **http://www.nelson.com/nelson.html**

All rights in this book are reserved.

ISBN 0-17-606559-8

**Canadian Cataloguing in Publication Data**

Kekewich, Jim
    Nelson Spelling 6

ISBN   0-17-606559-8

1. Spellers.    I. Kekewich, Deborah.    II. Title.

PE1145.2.K43 1996        428.1        C96-931467-1

Team Leader/Publisher: Mark Cobham
Project Editor: Jennifer Rowsell
Series Editors: Alan Simpson and Joanne Close
Series Designer: Peggy Rhodes
Cover Illustrator: Brian Hughes
Senior Composition Analyst: Marnie Benedict
Production Coordinator: Donna Brown
Permissions: Vicki Gould
Film: Imaging Excellence
Photography: Ray Boudreau

Printed and bound in Canada by Metropole Litho

**Acknowledgements**
Permission to reprint copyright material is gratefully acknowledged. Every reasonable effort to trace the copyright holders of materials appearing in this book has been made. Information that will enable the publisher to rectify any error or omission will be welcomed.

"Toad" by Valerie Worth from ALL THE SMALL POEMS © 1989. Published by Farrar, Straus & Giroux Inc.; "Breakaway" by Paul Yee, copyright © 1994. Published by Groundwood Books Ltd. Reprinted with permission; "Young Frankenstein's Robot Invention" by Berton Braley from LAUGHABLE LIMERICKS by Sara and John Brewton. Published by Thomas Y. Crowell; "i have looked" by Sonia Sanchez from I'VE BEEN A WOMAN by Sonia Sanchez. Reprinted with permission of Third World Press; "The Dream Keeper" by Langston Hughes from THE DREAM KEEPER AND OTHER POEMS by Langston Hughes. Copyright © 1932 and renewed 1960 by Langston Hughes. Reprinted by permission of Alfred A. Knopf, Inc.; "The Cow" by Arthur Guiterman from LYRIC LAUGHTER © 1939. Reprinted with permission of Louise H. Sclove; "The limerick's lively to write" by David McCord from TAKE SKY by David McCord. Copyright © 1961, 1962 by David McCord. By permission of Little, Brown and Company; "THE IMAGE-CARVERS" adapted from an article in *Equinox* magazine No. 49, 1990 by Barbara Brundege and Eugene Fisher.

**Illustrators**
Sean Dawdy, Suzanna Denti, Daniel Dumont, Norman Eyolfson, Sandy Nichols, Bill Suddick

**Reviewers**
The authors and publisher gratefully acknowledge the contributions of the following educators:

Halina Bartley
Peterborough, Ontario

Deborah Brandell
Edmonton, Alberta

Dena Domijan
Burnaby, British Columbia

Donna Duplak
Toronto, Ontario

Dr. Georgina Hedges
Grand Falls-Windsor, Newfoundland

Mary Passarelli
Toronto, Ontario

Lori Rog
Regina, Saskatchewan

Josephine Scott
Guelph, Ontario

Carolyn Sossi
Mississauga, Ontario

4 5   ML   01 00 99

# Table of Contents

# About Your Nelson Spelling Book

*Here are the features in your spelling book that will help you become a better speller.*

## Spelling Patterns

**2 Silent Consonants**

Each **Lesson** looks at a spelling pattern. A poem, short prose piece, or picture will show you some words that have the spelling pattern.

## Your Lesson Words

WORD MENU

passenger
reporter
forever
traveller
shutter
computer
member
clever
happier
hamster

In each lesson you will use the **Word Menu** to make a list of **Lesson Words** with the pattern you will be learning to spell. Sometimes we will include a few **challenge words** that we often find difficult to spell. You will be keeping your own **Personal Dictionary List** of words to use during your own reading, writing, and spelling.

## Working with Words

AT HOME

Activities, puzzles, and games will help you learn the meaning and spelling of words. You will practise your Lesson Words and learn new words. **CHALLENGE** announces an extra challenge you may want to try. You will be doing an activity at home. Sometimes you will be asking someone at home to help you.

## Spelling Strategies

STRATEGY SPOT

### Find a Word in a Word

The Strategy Spot in every lesson offers you ways to learn how to spell or proofread. Strategies are the tools that good spellers use. You can use these strategies when you are writing your own stories.

*The Writing Workshop* is a time to focus on a part of the writing process. In Writing Workshops you will learn techniques that writers use. You will practise these techniques in your writing and spelling classes.

## Grammar

# Focus on Language ▲ SENTENCE VARIETY

*Focus on Language* gives you information and activities on English grammar. You can use these activities during writing time.

### Connecting with ... Other Subjects

Here you will find activities that help you use spelling strategies in reading, writing, and completing projects in other school subjects.

### A Focus on Your Own Reading and Writing

*Connecting with Literature* activities and the poems and short prose pieces included throughout your book will let you study words in authentic reading situations.

i have looked into my father's eyes and seen an african sunset
— Sonia Sanchez

# Spell · Check   Every sixth lesson is a review of the spelling patterns and strategies you have been learning. You will be using the Lesson Words you still need to practise in games, puzzles, and other activities.

two   twice

QUICK TIP

*Quick Tips* will give you useful information and tips about patterns and meanings of words. You can use these tips right away in the lesson!

**DID YOU KNOW?** will tell you interesting information about how our language grew and how it works.

**FLASHBACK**

What strategy is most useful for you when you write words with silent consonants? Explain your choice.

*Flashback* is a quiet time at the end of each lesson to think over what you have learned.

*Spelling Stretch* is a special section of exciting games and challenges in the back of this book. Find out more about words and make your spelling skills stretch.

Spelling **S T R E T C H**

What do you think the message of this poem is?

**Toad**

When the flowers
Turned clever, and
Earned wide
Tender red petals
For themselves,

When the birds
Learned about feathers,
Spread green tails,
Grew cockades
On their heads,

The toad said:
Someone has got
To remember
The mud, and
I'm not proud.

— Valerie Worth

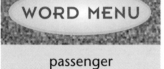

**WORD MENU**

passenger

reporter

forever

traveller

shutter

computer

member

clever

happier

hamster

lobster

diameter

photographer

producer

reviewer

# Creating Your Word List

**Say these words:**

| *reporter* | *shutter* | *clever* | *happier* |

What ending do these words share? What sound does the ending make?

1.  As a class, make a list of words that end in **-er**. The poem will help you. As you say each word out loud, STRESS the sound of **-er**.

2.  Work with your teacher to create the list of **-er** words you will be learning to spell. You can use: the Word Menu, the poem, your own words. These are your Lesson Words.

### 3. Writing Workshop

Look at the poem at the beginning of the lesson to see how the poet created images of birds. Select one animal and brainstorm a list of words that describe it. This is a good strategy to use when writing.

### 4. In your notebook

- Write each Lesson Word and underline the -**er** ending.
- A Personal Dictionary List will help in your reading and writing. Add -**er** words and other words you find interesting or challenging.

---

**STRATEGY SPOT**

## Remember the Rule — er Endings

There are exceptions to every spelling rule, but you can become a better speller if you remember what happens **most** of the time. For example, when you are trying to decide if you should use -**ur**, -**or**, -**ar**, or -**er** at the end of a word, remember:

- Many nouns that tell what people do end in -**er**. (teach**er**, review**er**)
- Many comparative adjectives end in -**er**. (bigg**er**, high**er**)

---

# Working with Words

### 1. Missing Letters    Fill in the missing letters in your notebook to write Word Menu words.

a) comput _ _    b) h _ _ s _ er    c) trave _ _ _ r

d) _ _ utter    e) rev _ _ _ er    f) l _ bs _ _ _

### 2. -er Occupations    We can add -**er** to some words to make the names of occupations (what people do). For example:

> write — A writ**er** is a person who writes.

Make new words by adding -**er**. Write the words in your notebook.

a) photograph    b) report    c) produce    d) office

CHALLENGE    Pick one of these jobs and brainstorm a list of words and phrases that describe this job.

AT HOME

### 3. Journal Entry    Write a journal entry about your day at school. Include a bold headline and a picture.

**4.** **Word Pole**   Copy and complete the Word Pole. Use the clues to write Word Menu words. When you are done, the word in the pole will name a person who elects someone.

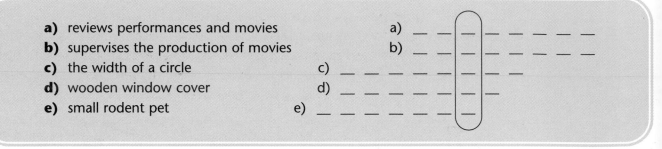

**a)** reviews performances and movies

**b)** supervises the production of movies

**c)** the width of a circle

**d)** wooden window cover

**e)** small rodent pet

a) _ _ | _ | _ _ _ _ _

b) _ _ | _ | _ _ _ _ _

c) _ _ _ _ _ _ | _ | _

d) _ _ _ _ _ | _ | _

e) _ _ _ _ _ _ _ _ _

**5.** **Word Definitions**   Choose 6 Lesson Words. Write a definition for each word, but do not include the word. For example, here is a definition of **passenger**: a person who rides in a car or other vehicle. Trade definitions with a partner and identify each other's 6 mystery words.

## QUICK TIP

The "**er**" sound can also be spelled **or**, **ir**, or **ur**. The patterns **ir** and **ur** are usually found in the middle of words.

● **DID YOU KNOW?**

All **verbs** that end in the **er** sound actually end with the letters **er** (**deliver, consider, remember,** and so on).

**6.** **Spelling Rules**   Write the spelling rule for each set of words that shows what happens when you add **-er**.

**a)** hit – hitter
run – runner

**b)** time – timer
compute – computer

**c)** high – higher
low – lower

**d)** carry – carrier
tangy – tangier

**7.** **Writing a Motto**   The Olympic motto is "Swifter, Higher, Stronger." Write a motto for your class. Design a banner for your motto.

# Focus on Language ▶ COMPARISON ADJECTIVES

An **adjective** can take 3 forms: **positive** (small), **comparative** (small**er**), **superlative** (small**est**). You can form most comparisons by adding -**er** or -**est** to adjectives or by using **more** or **most**. For one-syllable words, add -**er** or -**est**. For some two-syllable words, add -**er** or -**est**. Others need **more** or **most**. For three-syllable or longer words, add **more** or **most**. Some adjectives do not follow the rules; you just have to learn them. These are called **irregular adjectives**.

| positive | comparative | superlative |
|----------|-------------|-------------|
| long | longer | longest |
| tiny | tinier | tiniest |
| careful | more careful | most careful |
| good | better | best |
| little | less | least |

**1.** Copy the following chart and fill in the missing adjectives. Use a dictionary if you need help with irregular forms.

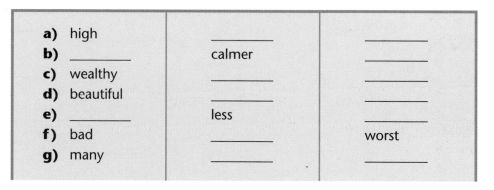

| | | |
|---|---|---|
| **a)** high | _____ | _____ |
| **b)** _____ | calmer | _____ |
| **c)** wealthy | _____ | _____ |
| **d)** beautiful | _____ | _____ |
| **e)** _____ | less | _____ |
| **f)** bad | _____ | worst |
| **g)** many | _____ | _____ |

**FLASHBACK**

How would you describe yourself as a speller? What are 2 things you would like to learn this year about spelling?

How many silent consonants can you find in this poem?

I have to say
my life's been dull
I've never known a gnu,
wrestled a knight,
talked to Tom Thumb,
or sat on a gnat or two.
I have never done
These things at all.
Tell me true —
Have you?

## WORD MENU

- √ calf
- √ limb
- √ crumb
- √ wrist
- √ knowledge
- √ knob
- √ climb
- √ wrinkle
- √ rhythm
- √ knit
- √ calm
- √ gnome
- √ soften
- √ ghastly

## Creating Your Word List

**Say these words:**

calf     wrist     knit     gnome

What is the same in these 4 words? All have **silent consonants**.

1.  As a class, make a list of words that have **silent consonants**. Use the poem to help you. Put the words into a chart like this:

| silent consonant at beginning | silent consonant in middle | silent consonant at end |
|---|---|---|
|  |  |  |

2.  Work with your teacher to create the list of **silent consonant** Lesson Words you will be learning to spell. You can use: the Word Menu, the poem, your own words.

3.  **In your notebook**
    - Write the Lesson Words. Circle the **silent consonants**.
    - Keep adding **silent consonant** words to your Personal Dictionary.

Saying the silent letters in words lets you know they are there (lim-**b**). But remember, silent letters are NOT pronounced in correct speech! Highlighting or capitalizing the silent letters can also help you remember them.

# Working with Words

1. **Say the Silent Letter**  Say all of your Lesson Words and pronounce the silent letters. Make a list of other silent letter words. Some will contain middle letters that we slide over (**kit**chen). Read aloud your list, stressing the silent letter.

2. **Sorting Silent Consonants**  Sort your Lesson Words by their silent consonants.

| kn- | gn- | -b | -l- | wr- | other |
|-----|-----|----|----|-----|-------|
|     |     |    |    |     |       |

CHALLENGE  Add 2 extra words to each column. Now answer these questions in your notebook:
  a) What type of letter comes before a pronounced **n**?
  b) What letter often comes before a silent **b**?
  c) What letter often comes after a silent **w**?

3. **Writing Homophones**  Drop the silent letter in each word to find a homophone. List the homophone pairs in your notebook. For example: **w**right – right.
  a) wring       b) wrote       c) wrap       d) wrack
  e) wrung       f) knew        g) wrest      h) write
  i) knight      j) knit        k) knot       l) two

CHALLENGE  Use 3 of the homophone pairs in sentences to show their meanings. Use a dictionary if you need help.

4. **Identifying Silent Letters**  Choose a short article in a magazine and list all the words that have silent consonants. Sort your words into groups according to the chart above.

## QUICK TIP

Thinking of related words can help you recall silent letters. Two belongs to the same family as twice and twins, in which you pronounce the **w**.

AT HOME

13

5. **Silent Code**   Copy the words below and circle the silent consonants. Transfer them to the corresponding number in the code. When you are finished, you will find the "colour of silence."

1. palm    2. autumn    3. scenes    4. calf
5. gnaw    6. column    7. fridge

6. **Word Stairs**   Write down a Lesson Word. Use the last letter of the word to start the next word. There's a catch: all your words must contain silent consonants! How far down can you make the stairs go? Stuck? Look in a dictionary.

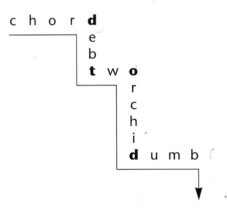

● *DID YOU KNOW ?*

Some silent letters were actually added to make word origin links more clear. The **g** was added to rei**g**n to link with the Latin *regnum*. The **b** was added to de**b**t to link with the Latin *debitum*.

7. **Writing Workshop**   You can use the format of an existing poem to form the basis of your own poem. Complete the line below and write your own poem like the one on page 12 to tell about YOUR life so far.

I have to say my life's been ...

FLASHBACK

What strategy is most useful for you when you write words with silent consonants? Explain your choice.

# Focus on Language ▶

Too much dialogue in a story can make it hard to read, but a little can add interest and excitement. You must punctuate dialogue correctly so it makes sense to a reader.

Quotation marks go around the words that were spoken aloud. A comma separates the quotation from the rest of the sentence. Here are some tips for punctuating with quotation marks:

- Always put commas inside quotation marks.
  "I think we should leave," said Eli.

- When a quotation mark ends a sentence, place the period inside the quotation marks.
  Kira answered, "In a minute."

- Exclamation points and question marks go inside only if they are part of the quotation.

- Begin a new paragraph for each new speaker's words.
  "I think we should leave," said Eli.
  Kira answered, "In a minute."
  "Well," Mai yelled, "I'm all set!"

What do you notice about the first letter of the first word in each quotation?

**1.** Copy and punctuate this dialogue. Be sure to start a new paragraph each time a new person speaks.

> Last night I spent 8 hours on spelling said May. Wow said Fay it's great that you spent so much time studying! Who said anything about studying answered May I put my spelling book under the mattress when I went to bed!

**CHALLENGE** Draw cartoon boxes like the ones below and fill in the speech balloons to create a comic strip.

What would your mom or dad do if you brought this dog home?

FOR SALE — Playful, beautiful St. Bernard. Boundless energy, harmless — likes all people, including young children. Requires loving home, plentiful, meatless diet (strict vegetarian), and a big yard. For more information, call (555) BIG-DOGS.

How many **suffixes** can you find in this ad?

## WORD MENU

peaceful
hopeful
wonderful
successful
timeless
hopeless
effortless
careful
harmful
harmless
worthless
motionless

## Creating Your Word List

**Say these words:**
The **suffix -ful** can mean "full of" or "able to."
Say the new word created when the **suffix -ful** is added to:

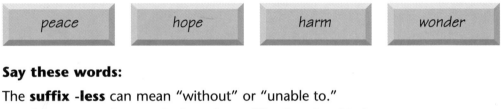

| peace | hope | harm | wonder |

**Say these words:**
The **suffix -less** can mean "without" or "unable to."
Say the new word created when the **suffix -less** is added to:

| hope | time | harm | worth |

1. As a class, make a list of words that end in **-ful** and **-less**.

2. Work with your teacher to create the list of **-ful** and **-less** words you will be learning to spell. You can use: the Word Menu, the ad above, your own words.
   Include these 3 **challenge words** in your Lesson Words:

   **beautiful, people, heard**

   **Challenge words** are words that most people find difficult to spell.

3. **In your notebook**
   • Write each Lesson Word and underline the suffix.
   • Add **-ful** and **-less** words and **challenge words** to your Personal Dictionary list. Keep it up to date.

## Find a Word in a Word

To remember the spelling of words, find smaller words in them. For example, the word **hear** is in **heard**. In **favourite**, you can find **favour** and **our**. Find the smaller words in each of your Lesson Words.

# Working with Words

**1. Noting Syllables**   Write your Lesson Words, using a coloured hyphen (-) to break up the **syllables**. For example: won-der-ful.

**2. Words in Words**   Which Word Menu words contain these small words? Write each small word and the word(s) it's in.
   **a)** pea          **b)** or          **c)** hop          **d)** won

**3. Adding Consonants**   Complete the words in your notebook, adding the missing **consonants**.
   **a)**  _ eo _ _ e          **b)**  _ ea _ _
   **c)**  _ u _ _ e _ _ _ u _          **d)**  _ o _ _ e _ _ u _
   **e)**  _ o _ e _ u _          **f)**  e _ _ o _ _ _ e _ _
   **g)**  _ i _ e _ e _ _          **h)**  _ eau _ _ _ u _

   Which words were the easiest to complete? Why?

**4. Word Formulas**   Use the meaning clues and word math to write Word Menu words.
   **a)** "quick jump" + e + less =
   **b)** ef + "defensive building" + less =
   **c)** "opposite of she" + lp + less =
   **d)** "finished first" + der + ful =
   **e)** "a clock's message" + less =

   **CHALLENGE**   Make up 3 of your own word formulas. Use Lesson Words and other words you can spell.

**5. Word Explosion**   "Explode" 3 of the words below by adding **prefixes** and **suffixes**. Write as many new words as you can. You can use a dictionary.
   **a)** beauty          **b)** play          **c)** harm          **d)** thought
   **e)** help          **f)** hope          **g)** breath          **h)** care

motionless

QUICK TIP

The spelling of a word does not usually change when we add **-ful** or **-less**. An exception is words that end in **-y**. We change the final **y** to **i** before adding the **suffix**.

**6. Word Pole**  Copy and complete this Word Pole. Use the word meanings to write Lesson Words. When you are done, the word in the pole will answer the question, "What do all of these words do?"

**a)** great, awesome       a) _ _ _ | _ _ _ _ _

**b)** calm                      b) _ | _ _ _ _ _ _

**c)** given up        c) _ _ _ _ _ | _ _

**d)** cautious                   d) _ | _ _ _ _ _ _

**e)** very easy        e) _ _ | _ _ _ _ _ _

**f)** lasting forever            f) _ | _ _ _ _ _ _

**g)** very pretty                g) _ | _ _ _ _ _ _ _

**h)** does not hurt   h) _ _ _ _ _ | _ _

**7. Word Pyramid**  Choose a Lesson Word you need to practise. Draw a triangle in your notebook. At the top, print the first letter of the word. On the second line, print the first 2 letters. On the third line, print the first 3 letters. Continue until the triangle is full. Build a word pyramid for each of your 3 **challenge words**.

> ● **DID YOU KNOW ?**
> The **suffix -ful** can mean "enough to fill." You find this meaning in recipe words like **teaspoonful** and **cupful**. These words are **nouns**, NOT **adjectives**.

**8. Changing Nouns to Adjectives**  The suffixes **-ful** and **-less** turn **nouns** into **adjectives**. Complete this chart in your notebook using 10 nouns that can take either **-ful** or **-less**. A thesaurus will give you some ideas.

| noun | adjective |
| --- | --- |
| effort | effortless |

**AT HOME**

**9. Personal Narrative**  Using your Lesson Words, write a description of yourself. Use phrases like:

I am careful when ...       I have been successful at ...

# Focus on Language  SIMILES AND METAPHORS

You can write comparisons of 2 unlike things. A **simile** compares one thing to another by using the words **like** or **as**:

> The waves were like galloping horses.

A **metaphor** compares one thing to another more directly, without using **like** or **as**:

The waves were galloping horses.

1. Complete these **similes** using your own ideas. Avoid **clichés** (overused expressions). For example, instead of writing "cold as ice," you could write "cold as metal in winter."
   a) as effortless as …       b) as peaceful as …
   c) as graceful as …         d) walked like …
   e) ran like …               f) fell like …
   g) as motionless as …       h) as timeless as …

2. Use a **metaphor** to complete each sentence below. Add any other words you need so that your meaning is clear.
   a) The thunder was …        b) The moon was …
   c) The clouds were …        d) The noisy children were …
   e) The rain was …           f) The trees were …

3. **Writing Workshop**
   You can use **similes** and **metaphors** in your own story writing. Brainstorm some similes and metaphors you might use in a story.

4. Illustrate one of the **similes** or **metaphors** you have created or read. Compare your illustration with a classmate's.

FLASHBACK

How can using prefixes and suffixes make your writing more interesting?

Read these 2 opening paragraphs. What do you learn about the characters, setting, and plot of the novel?

> The Model T lurched and shuddered to a stop. Kwok-Ken Wong could hear the rain drumming steadily onto the canvas roof above and into the big tin tubs on the truck's open deck. Water dripped from the fire-escape ladder hanging on the nearby building and washed over the cobblestones down towards the sewer. The storm had driven the scavenging cats indoors and capped the dank smells of garbage.
>
> Kwok scanned the alley with anxious eyes. The laneway stood empty. He breathed with relief. Still, he sank lower into the hard, well-worn seat. Once, two teenage girls had come chasing through, laughing and giggling. They had stopped when they saw Kwok working....
>
> — from *Breakaway* by Paul Yee

Reread the novel excerpt and note all the words that end in **-ed**.

**WORD MENU**

advanced
annoyed
arranged
blurred
chuckled
copied
collected
created
divided
drowned
buried
delivered
invited

## Creating Your Word List

**Say these words:**

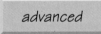

| advanced | copied | invited |

What sound does **-ed** make in each word? The word part **-ed** is a **suffix**. When you add the **suffix -ed** to the end of a verb, you make the **past tense** (happen**ed** in the past).

1. List words that have the **suffix -ed**. The novel excerpt above will help you. Read the words out loud and pay attention to the sound of **-ed** in each word.

2. Work with your teacher to create the list of **-ed** words you will be learning to spell. You can use: the Word Menu, the excerpt, your own words. Include these 2 **challenge words** in your Lesson Words:

   **grabbed, started**

**3. In your notebook**
- Write the Lesson Words and underline the **suffix -ed**.
- Keep adding **-ed** words to your Personal Dictionary.

## Does It Look Right?

Sometimes you can't rely on the sound of a word for its spelling. It helps to have a sense of whether it looks right. If you're not sure, write the word 2 ways. The one that looks right probably is.

# Working with Words

**1. Add -ing**   Write the **root word** for each word. Then add **-ing** to each word and write the new words.
   a) arranged      b) blurred      c) buried      d) created
   e) divided      f) delivered      g) invited      h) grabbed

**2. Proofreading Practice**   Pick the correct spelling in each row. Then use each word in an interesting sentence. Use your proofreading strategies to check each sentence.
   a) copyed, coppied, copied, kopied
   b) unoyed, anoyed, annoied, annoyed
   c) arrangied, arranged, aranged, arrannged

**3. Double Up**   List the words from the Word Menu that double the final consonant before adding **-ed**. Underline the double consonant. What other words can you add to the list?

**QUICK TIP**

Words ending in **x** are exceptions; they stay the same when suffixes are added: fix**ed**, fix**er**, fix**ing**. Words ending in double consonants stay the same (**adding**).

**4. Verb Tenses**   Words ending in **-ed** are often the past tense of verbs. Complete this chart in your notebook.

| Past | Present | Future |
| --- | --- | --- |
| a) buried | bury | will bury |
| b) delivered | _____ | _____ |
| c) _____ | grab | _____ |
| d) started | _____ | _____ |
| e) _____ | invite | _____ |
| f) arranged | _____ | _____ |

**AT HOME**

**5.** **More Than One** Ask people at home to describe their day. Get them to keep talking until they say at least 5 **-ed** words. Record these **-ed** words in alphabetical order.

**6.** **What's My Rule?** Read over each group of words. Match each group of words to the rule it follows when **-ed** is added.

> **a)** Drop **e** and add **-ed**.
> **b)** Change **y** to **i**.
> **c)** Double the final consonant.
> **d)** Just add **-ed**.

**1** bury/buried, fry/fried, copy/copied
**2** blur/blurred, grab/grabbed, step/stepped
**3** collect/collected, annoy/annoyed, advance/advanced
**4** divide/divided, create/created, copy/copied

**7.** **Exploding Words!** "Explode" the words below by adding **-s**, **-ed**, **-ing**, **un-**, and so on. Check spellings in a dictionary.
**a)** copy **b)** collect **c)** invite **d)** divide

**8.** **Descriptive Synonyms** Use a dictionary or thesaurus to help you replace each underlined word with a more descriptive synonym.
  a) I walked to the store.
  b) I rode down the street on my bike.
  c) Tam jumped over the fence.
  d) They looked across the field.
  e) James found a magic urn.

Look through your writing folder or journal. Are there any overused words you can replace?

**9.** **Writing Workshop** Reread the 2 opening paragraphs on page 20. Notice how the verbs **lurched**, **shuddered**, and **scanned** make the writing come alive. With a partner, write an excerpt from a novel — real or imagined. Make your excerpt as lively as possible by using descriptive verbs. Share your excerpt with your classmates. Based on what you have written, would they like to read the book?

# Focus on Language  SUBJECT–VERB AGREEMENT

Every sentence has a subject and a verb. A **singular** (one) **subject** takes a **singular verb**. A **plural** (more than one) **subject** takes a **plural verb**. Here are 5 special situations you can check whenever you are in doubt.

1.  Make the verb agree with its subject, not necessarily the nearest noun:

    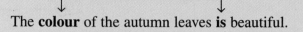

    The **colour** of the autumn leaves **is** beautiful.

2.  Watch out for nouns that end in **-s** but are singular:

    The **news was** not good yesterday.

3.  When the subject of the sentence is made up of 2 or more singular nouns joined by the word **and**, use a plural verb:

    Sarah **and** Ali **have** joined our team.

4.  Nouns that name a group (collective nouns like **group**, **team**, **bunch**, **crowd**, **family**) usually take a singular verb:

    A **bunch** of grapes **was** glued to the display.

5.  Indefinite pronouns ending in **-one**, **-body**, and **-thing** take a singular verb:

    **Everyone loves** my pet.

Copy the 5 guidelines above in your notebook. Write at least 1 more example sentence for each guideline. Exchange sample sentences with a partner and check that each other's sentences are correct.

### FLASHBACK

Do you feel more confident as a writer and speller? If not, what will you do to help yourself?

Enjoy this limerick about a famous fictional monster.

> Young Frankenstein's robot invention
> Caused trouble too awful to mention.
>> Its actions were ghoulish,
>> Which proves it is foolish
>> To monkey with nature's intention.

Which words in the poem have the sound of **"shun"**?

## WORD MENU

education
concentration
production
conversation
direction
information
selection
competition
introduction
addition
composition
animation
collection
combination

## Creating Your Word List

- **Say these words:**

| selection | production | direction |

What sound does the ending **-tion** make?

- **Say these words:**

| competition | addition | information | education |

Notice that in some words a vowel is added before the **-tion** ending.

**1.** As a class, make a list of words that end in **-tion**, **-ition**, and **-ation**. Put the words into a chart like this:

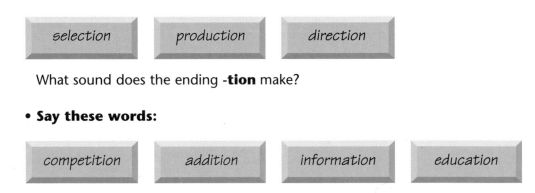

| -tion | -ition | -ation |
| --- | --- | --- |
|  |  |  |

**2.** Work with your teacher to create the list of **"shun"** words you will be learning to spell. You can use: the Word Menu, the limerick, your own words. Include this **challenge word** in your Lesson Words:

**pollution**

### 3. In your notebook
- Write each Lesson Word and underline the **"shun"** ending.
- Keep adding new **"shun"** words and **challenge words** to your Personal Dictionary list. Keep it up to date.

**STRATEGY SPOT**

## Look for Similar Letter Patterns

To help yourself spell new words, look for a common letter pattern. For example, in this lesson **all** of your words end in **-ion**, so all you really have to focus on are the word beginnings.

# Working with Words

**1. Scrambled Syllables** Put these Word Menu words back together and write them in your notebook.

| | | | | | | |
|---|---|---|---|---|---|---|
| edu | | di | | | | |
| sel | | ima | | | | |
| pro | | rec | | | | |
| col | + | bina | + | tion | = | **?** |
| ad | | duc | | | | |
| di | | lec | | | | |
| an | | ca | | | | |
| com | | ec | | | | |

**2. Strategy Practice** Use the spelling strategy above to practise 4 words you find challenging to spell.

**3. Changing Verbs to Nouns** When you add a **"shun"** ending to a word, it often changes a **verb** (action word) into a **noun** (person, place, or thing). Write the **verbs** that form the base of each of your Lesson Words. For example, the verb "to compose" forms the base of **composition**.

**QUICK TIP**

Words that end in **-de** and **-se** drop the **-de** and **-se** before adding **-sion** (divi**de** – divi**sion**, ten**se** – ten**sion**).

**4. Adding -tion** Write the root word of each of the following words. Beside each root word, write the letters that are deleted when adding **-tion**.

a) connection
b) introduction
c) selection
d) contribution
e) instruction
f) concentration

**5. Word Meanings** This game is like "I spy" except that you give definitions for **-tion** words and your partner **spells** the answer. For example: "I'm thinking of a word that means people talking." "Is it **c-o-n-v-e-r-s-a-t-i-o-n**?" Take turns.

**6. Writing Workshop** When you give information, you can do it in many ways: chart, diagram, sentences, point form. Choose a topic you are studying and present information on it in 2 of these ways.

**7. Adding -ition and -ation** Write the root word of each of the following words. Beside each root word, write the letter that is dropped when adding **-ition** or **-ation**.
  a) competition      b) animation      c) composition
  d) conversation     e) education      f) combination

   **CHALLENGE** What part of speech is each root word in questions **4** and **7**?

---

● *DID YOU KNOW?*

**Fashion** and **cushion** are the only English words that end in **-shion**. Words ending in **-sian** and **-tian** are usually names of nationalities (A**sian**). No English word actually ends in **-shun**!

---

AT HOME

**8. Writing Directions** Write the **directions** on how to go from your home to your school.

**9. Word Explosion** Watch the word **educate** "explode"!

educates
educated          educate          education
                                   uneducated
                                   educating

Explode these words. Use a dictionary to check your words.
  a) add      b) direct      c) inform

---

FLASHBACK

What new "shun" words have you learned in this lesson?

## ations

If we meet and I say, "Hi,"

That's a salutation.

If you ask me how I feel,

That's consideration.

If we stop and talk awhile,

That's a conversation.

If we understand each other,

That's communication.

If we argue, scream and fight,

That's an altercation.

If later we apologize,

That's reconciliation.

If we help each other home,

That's cooperation.

And all these ations added up

Make civilization.

(And if I say this is a wonderful
    poem,

Is that exaggeration?)

— Shel Silverstein

1. Discuss, with a partner, the meaning of each **-ation** word the poet used. If you're stumped by a word, look for its root and at the words around it that give clues to its meaning. Check your guess in a dictionary.

2. Reread the poem, but this time focus on each verse (sentence). Can you write another verse using either **education** or **concentration**?

3. Work with a partner to mime 2 or 3 verses of the poem.

use your imagination

# Spell·Check

**Patterns**

-er
silent consonants
suffixes -less, -ful
suffix -ed
-tion

**Strategies**

1. Remember the rule — er endings.
2. Say the silent letters.
3. Find a word in a word.
4. Does it look right?
5. Look for similar letter patterns.

## Creating Your Word List

**In your notebook**

- Go to your list of "Words I Still Need to Practise."
- Pick 15 words you need to practise spelling. These are your Review Lesson Words.

## Working with Words

1. **Highlighting Silent Letters**  Write your Review Lesson Words. Highlight any silent letters you find. Say each word, pronouncing silent letters to help you remember the spelling.

2. **Finding Letter Patterns**  Look for common letter patterns in your Review Lesson Words. If you find 2 or more that match, circle them with a coloured pencil. Use a different colour for each pattern.

3. **Spelling Bookmark**  Make a decorated bookmark to help keep your place in this spelling book.

4. **Word Web**  Copy and complete this Word Web. Draw a detailed picture or a 6-frame comic to illustrate your web.

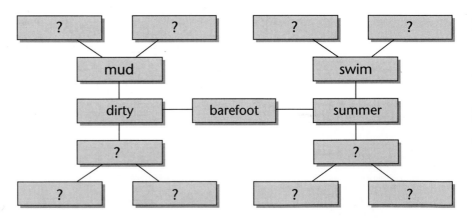

AT HOME

5. **Strategy Review**  Use the spelling strategies in the last 5 lessons to study your Review Lesson Words.

**6. Word Chain**  See how long a Word Chain you can make. Write down a Review Lesson Word. Use the last letter of that word to start the next word from your list. For example:

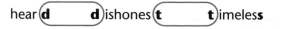

hear **d** **d**ishones **t** **t**imeles**s**

Use other words you know how to spell to continue the chain.

**7. Word Mountain**  To make a Word Mountain, print a small word at the top. Underneath add another word that is longer **and** follows alphabetically. Make 3 mountains starting with **be**, **so**, and **we**.

he
hem
hide
hockey
hopping

**8. Forming Compounds**  These words are worth points. Put them together to make **compound words**.

rail = 12    house = 7    sail = 8    every = 3    day = 9    thing = 2
road = 11    row = 10    boat = 4    one = 6    body = 5    some = 1

Which word has the highest total? Which has the lowest? Which have the same total?

*Proofreading Spotlight*

### Scan Back!

It is difficult to proofread your own work. Your mind knows what the words are supposed to say — it does most of the work while your eyes go on "autopilot." Here's a tip. Read your work backwards! This way the story makes no sense to your mind, so your eyes have to look at each individual word. For example, to proofread the sentence **"Our family's dog is called Miller"** you would read the words in this order: **Miller called is dog family's Our**.
*Proofread your last story or journal entry using Scan Back: start at the bottom, and read each sentence backwards to the top.*

**FLASHBACK**

Have a partner dictate your 15 Review Lesson Words. Correct any words you spelled incorrectly. Cross off your list the words you spelled correctly. Bravo! You're doing a great job.

What pictures do you see in your mind as you read this poem?

> There were sunny days, without a cloud in the sky.
> When I dived in the lake, my senses came alive.
> Moving through the water, I felt really free.
> No worries, as the waves gently washed over me.

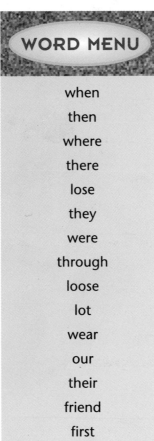

**WORD MENU**

when

then

where

there

lose

they

were

through

loose

lot

wear

our

their

friend

first

## Creating Your Word List

The words in the Word Menu are common words called **sight words**. They are quickly recognized on sight, but easily misspelled. Although they are short, common words, each word is a **challenge word**. **Challenge words** are words that most people find difficult to spell.

**1.** As a class, make a list of common words you find a challenge to spell.

**2.** Work with your teacher to create the list of **challenge words** you will be learning to spell. You can use: the Word Menu, your own words. These are your Lesson Words.

**3. In your notebook**
- Write each Lesson Word and <u>underline</u> the part that you need to practise.
- Say each word and imagine the word in your mind.
- You may want to add some of these words to your Personal Dictionary. Keep this list up to date to help in your reading and writing.

## Working with Words

**1. Fancy Letters**   Look at the words from the Word Menu that gave you problems. Softly say each word to yourself. Print each word using fancy letters.

**2. Rhyming Words**   Write a word that rhymes with each Lesson Word.

## Visualize Words

When you visualize a word, you "see" in your mind what the word looks like.

**1.** Write down a Lesson Word.

**2.** Cover it with a piece of paper.

**3.** Imagine you can still see the word. Try to get a picture of it in your mind.

**4.** Uncover the word. Did you visualize it correctly?

Try this strategy with 6 of your Lesson Words.

---

**3. Alphabetizing** Write your Lesson Words in alphabetical order.

**4. Antonyms** Find 2 words that are **antonyms** (opposite in meaning) of each of these words:

**a)** lose  **b)** first  **c)** friend  **d)** loose

**CHALLENGE** Use 1 pair of antonyms in the SAME sentence.

**5. Homophones** Pick 3 homophone pairs and use each pair in a sentence. For example:

**to/too** — I was **too** sick **to** play in the soccer game.

**a)** their/there  **b)** where/wear  **c)** our/hour
**d)** its/it's  **e)** passed/past  **f)** threw/through

**CHALLENGE** Find at least 2 of your own homophone pairs or trios. Add them to your class list of homophones.

**6. Wordprints** A **footprint** shows the shape of a foot. A **wordprint** shows the shape of a word. Draw the wordprint shape of each of your Lesson Words. For example:

**7. Spelling Tic-Tac-Toe** Each person must use a different-coloured pencil. Player A prints a Lesson Word in 1 square on a tic-tac-toe board. Player B then prints a Lesson Word on the same tic-tac-toe board. Keep adding words until a player completes 3 words in a row.

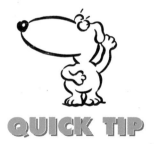

**QUICK TIP**

Knowing which **homophone** to use can be tricky. Make sure that you listen very carefully to the sentence so that you'll know which word to use.

31

**8. Then There Were None**   Try to use ALL the letters in the box only once to make words. Copy the letters and erase each letter when it is used. You may want to play with a partner.

```
t t h a p n w e l
r h o e l r e a
```

**AT HOME**

**9. Graphing Word Use**   Find a short newspaper article. Count the number of times each of your Lesson Words appears. Make a graph to show your results. Which words were used the most?

**10. Word Analogies**   Use the Word Menu to figure out these word analogies. Write the completed sentences in your notebook.
   a) **Up** is to **down** as **here** is to _____ .
   b) **He** is to **him** as _____ is to **them**.
   c) **Bicycle** is to **ride** as **clothes** are to _____ .
   d) **Broken** is to **fix** as _____ is to **tighten**.

● *DID YOU KNOW?*

In 1971, yellow smiley-face buttons were everywhere. And it seemed that everyone was saying the slogan that went with them: "Have a nice day!" The smiley button and its slogan were originally part of an ad campaign for a New York City radio station.

**11. Word Web**   Write the word **friend**. What 2 words does it make you think of? What other words does each new word make you think of? Add as many words as you can to make a Word Web. See page 28 for an example of a Word Web.

   **CHALLENGE**   Use your Word Web as the basis of a story or poem you write at home.

**12. Same Spelling**   Some words are spelled the same but have different meanings and different pronunciations. For example:

   Please **close** the door. I am too **close** to the cliff's edge.
   I listened to the **record**. Please **record** your answers.

Make a list of similar word pairs. Give the meaning for each word in the pair.

# Focus on Language  CAPITAL LETTERS

Use capital letters for the:

| | |
|---|---|
| • first word in a sentence | **B**ring me my coat. |
| • names of people | **L**isa **C**heng, **M**om, **I** |
| • names of places | **W**innipeg, **N**ational **G**allery |
| • months, days, and holidays | **M**arch, **T**uesday, **E**aster |
| • titles of books, songs, films | **N**elson **S**pelling |

**1.** Write the names of 2 places you would like to visit. Write the names of 3 holidays you enjoy. Then write the names of 3 books, songs, or films you have enjoyed and share your response with a partner.

**2.** Correct these sentences by adding capital letters.
   **a)** maria and david will come with me to the canadian museum of civilization.
   **b)** sarah went to florida last january.
   **c)** st. john's is the capital city of newfoundland.
   **d)** this friday, october 31, is hallowe'en.

**3.** Write a short note to a partner. Leave out all of the capitals. Try to include a few different usages. Your partner has to send you back your note with all the capital corrections.

meet joey and i at the viewmaster cinema
at 4:00 p.m. tuesday. be sure to b̶ ̶ ̶

**4.** Find and list 15 words with capital letters for people, places, or particular things in your neighbourhood.

**5. Writing Workshop**
Your community is a topic you know a lot about! Use your community as the writing topic in one of your writing classes.

FLASHBACK

How does the visualization strategy help you in your everyday life?

Let's look at three definitions from the dictionary. Notice all the things the dictionary tells about each word:

**prefix** (prē′ fiks) *n.* letters added at the beginning of a word to change its meaning: *When you put the prefix "pre-" in front of the word "historic." you get "prehistoric."* pl. **prefixes**.

**interjection** (in′ tər jek′ shen) *n.* an exclamation or cry of emotion: *Some interjections are "Oh!" "Ah!" and "Ouch!"*

**refresh** (ri fresh′) *v.* **refreshes**. **refreshed**. to make fresh again or to give new strength: *Refresh yourself by taking a nap.*

## WORD MENU

preview
precaution
prepare
interact
interfere
international
interview
review
rewrite
refill
reproduce
reopen
recycle
request
represent

## Creating Your Word List

**Say these words:**

• Say the new word created when the **prefix pre-** is added to:

**view, heat, pay**

The **prefix pre-** means "before" (**pre**heat — heat before).

• Say the new word created when the **prefix inter-** is added to:

**view, act, national**

The **prefix inter-** means "between" (**inter**national — between nations).

• Say the new word created when the **prefix re-** is added to:

**view, open, pay**

The **prefix re-** can mean "again" (reopen — open again) or "back" (**re**pay — pay back). What does review mean?

**1.** Make a list of words that use these prefixes. Put them into a chart:

| pre- | inter- | re- |
| --- | --- | --- |
|  |  |  |

**2.** Work with your teacher to create the list of **pre-**, **inter-**, and **re-** Lesson Words you will be learning to spell. You can use: the Word Menu, the definitions, your own words.

**3. In your notebook**
- Write the Lesson Words and highlight the **prefixes**.
- Add **pre-**, **inter-**, and **re-** words to your Personal Dictionary.

## Look for Prefixes and Suffixes

Knowing the meanings and spellings of **prefixes** and **suffixes** can help you spell larger words. Think about the root word. If you already know how to spell it, add the prefix or suffix. If you don't, use strategies to spell the root word, check your spelling, then add the prefix or suffix.

# Working with Words

**1. Adding Prefixes**   Add **pre-** or **re-** to each word:

| Before | Now | Again/Back |
|--------|-----|------------|
| a) _____ | pay | b) _____ |
| c) _____ | view | d) _____ |
| e) _____ | write | f) _____ |

**2. Replace and Rewrite**   Rewrite this paragraph by replacing the **bold** words with just 1 word starting with **pre-**, **inter-**, or **re-**. The Word Menu will help you.

My new pen doesn't work! All yesterday's schoolwork had to be **written again**. I spilled the ink on my work when the pen needed to be **filled again**. When the store **opens again**, I am going to **ask politely** that the owner **give back** my money or give me another pen to **take the place of** the faulty pen.

**3. Writing Acronyms**   Practise using **acronyms**. Give a partner 3 letters. Ask your partner to make up words that begin with the letters. Try to form a phrase or a short sentence. For example **BFD** = **b**eautifully **f**lying **d**oves.

prepare

## QUICK TIP

Pay attention to the **meanings** of words when you look for prefixes and suffixes. Some words look as if they start with a prefix but do not. **Prepare** uses the prefix **pre-**, but **preach** does not.

**4. Adding Prefix inter-** Add the prefix **inter-** to whatever root words you can to make real words.

| | | | | | |
|---|---|---|---|---|---|
| change | lace | phone | national | twine | lock |
| act | section | board | stellar | play | key |

CHALLENGE  Illustrate 4 of these new words.

**5. Writing Workshop** Before you rewrite a story, it sometimes helps to talk about it with someone. Try this with a story you are working on. This is called a **Story Preview**.

**6. Listing Personal Preferences** What are some things you like to do, and some that you dislike doing? Can you think of 5 for each list?

CHALLENGE  Use your lists as the basis for a story or poem.

AT HOME

**7. Finding re- Words** What jobs or actions are continually repeated at home? Ask someone to help you make a list. Use the **prefix re-**. For example: **Re**open the fridge.

● *DID YOU KNOW?*

The **Internet** is a global cooperative network of university, corporate, government, and private computers communicating with each other over telephone lines. Computers on the Internet can exchange data quickly with each other to download files and send E-mail. The word comes from **inter**national and **net**work.

**8. Concentration** Cut a sheet of paper into 20 equal-sized squares. Write your Lesson Words twice — 1 word per square. Turn the squares over, and mix them up. Number the **back** of the squares from 1 to 20. Take turns turning over 2 numbers until you get a pair of matching words.

FLASHBACK

Think about all of the prefixes you know so far. Do you remember how each one changes the meaning of a word?

# Connecting with

# SCIENCE

## ABC Organizers

These organizers can help you keep track of words that you meet and use in science units. At the beginning of each unit, make a chart like the one shown below. Each square should be large enough that you can record several words in it. To help you get started, here is the first section of an ABC Organizer for an environment unit.

| A B C ORGANIZER: The Environment by Joseph Lee | | | | A acid rain | B biodegradable |
|---|---|---|---|---|---|
| C conserve | D disaster | E environment | F forestry | G Greenpeace | H |
| I | J | K | L | M | N |
| O | P | Q | R | S | T |
| U | V | W | X | Y | Z |

Sources of words for your organizer can include books you read, videos you watch, field trips you experience, and presentations you hear. You can include related people, places, things, ideas, concepts, and areas of study.

For each unit, try to record 1 word in each square. (Warning: X and Z can be difficult so don't worry if you can't find related words.) After you have written a word, check to make sure you have spelled the word correctly. Keep all of your organizers. At the end of the year, you can make an individual science dictionary or work with your classmates to make a class science dictionary.

# Suffixes -ent, -ence

Enjoy this haiku poem.

> Ancient pines swaying
> Silently brushing the sky
> Fervent shadows dance

Reread the poem. Notice the word endings and the number of syllables in each line.

## WORD MENU

permanent

ancient

decent

absent

event

prevent

silent

intelligence

confidence

evidence

represent

current

element

silence

obedience

## Creating Your Word List

**Say these words:**

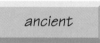

| ancient | absent |

What sound do you hear? The final unstressed syllable sound is "ənt" which is spelled **-ent**. The symbol "ə" is an unstressed vowel called a **schwa**.

**Say these words:**

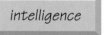

| intelligence | evidence |

What sound do you hear? The final unstressed syllable sound "ənce" is spelled **-ence**.

**1.** As a class, make a list of words that end in **-ent** and **-ence**. Put the words into a chart like this:

| -ent | -ence |
|------|-------|
|      |       |

**2.** Work with your teacher to create the list of "ənt" and "ənce" words you will be learning to spell. You can use: the Word Menu, the poem, your own words. These are your Lesson Words.

### 3. In your notebook

- Write each Lesson Word and circle the letters that make up the "ənt"/"əncə" ending.
- Keep adding "ənt"/"əncə" words to your Personal Dictionary list. Keep it up to date.

## Feel the Rhythm

If you get to know a word's **rhythm** it helps you spell it. You can do this by saying or singing the word as you tap your foot, snap your fingers, or clap your hands to show its **syllables**.

# Working with Words

**1. Writing Workshop**   Apply the information presented in the "Strategy Spot" to help you write a poem. Say or sing each word you would like to include in your poem. Keeping beat makes you more aware of syllables in the word and can help you decide to keep or reject it.

**2. Categorizing Words**   Copy and complete this category chart with words containing the required number of syllables.

|  | 1 syllable | 2 syllables | 3 syllables | 4 syllables |
|---|---|---|---|---|
| school subjects | gym | spelling | history | mathematics |
| vegetables | a) | b) | c) | d) |
| insects | e) | f) | g) | h) |
| mammals | i) | j) | k) | l) |
| countries | m) | n) | o) | p) |
| sports | q) | r) | s) | t) |

**3. -ent Antonyms**   Use your dictionary or thesaurus to help you find a word that means the opposite and ends in **-ent** for:

a) present      b) argument      c) decent

`CHALLENGE`   Use each word and its antonym in the same sentence.

**QUICK TIP**

If the stress is placed on the last syllable in a word ending in a **vowel + r**, the ending is spelled **ence** (oc**cur** – occur**rence**, pre**fer** – prefer**ence**).

AT HOME

4.  **Sentence Beginnings**   Write 5 sentence beginnings using your Lesson Words. For example:

    Maria saw evidence of ...

5.  **Noting Syllables**   Try out the strategy with your Lesson Words, as you exaggerate the pronunciation of each one.

6.  **Sorting Words**   Write each Lesson Word on a card. Think of different ways of sorting your words: by meaning, by part of speech, by spelling pattern, by number of letters. Sort your words 5 different ways.

7.  **Illustrate the Poem**   Illustrate the haiku poem on page 38. Try to convey its mood.

## ● DID YOU KNOW?

There are no rules that will help us tell when to use **-ent** or **-ence**. We have to memorize these words or use a dictionary. That's because these words and their endings come from ways of forming verbs in Latin.

| | |
|---|---|
| -tion | un- |
| -ly | -ed |
| -ful | -ial |
| re- | -tive |
| -ing | -ance |
| -ence | mis- |

8.  **Adding Prefixes and Suffixes**   Add as many prefixes and suffixes from the box as you can to each word below to make a "family" of words. What part of speech is each new word in the family? Three parts of speech in a family is average. You may have to make some changes to the root word. Do it like this:

    current       —   **adjective**
    currently     —   **adverb**
    currency      —   **noun**

    **a)** represent   **b)** deliver   **c)** silent   **d)** decent
    **e)** absent      **f)** event     **g)** confident   **h)** permanent

### FLASHBACK

Look back at the activities in this lesson. Which one helped you the most?

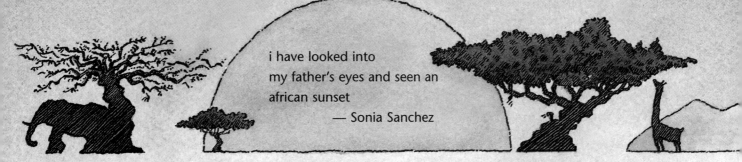

i have looked into
my father's eyes and seen an
african sunset
— Sonia Sanchez

## Haiku

This poem is called a **haiku**. Haiku was invented in Japan hundreds of years ago. Haiku has a definite structure and purpose:

- It has 3 lines, with
- 5 syllables in the first line
- 7 in the second
- 5 again in the third

Haiku is a simple statement describing an emotion or something in nature. Note that the poet has used lowercase letters instead of capitals. This is not a standard feature of haiku. Many poets choose to use unconventional punctuation and capitalization.

1. Look through books and magazines to find pictures of animals or scenes of nature. Choose one that inspires you and write a haiku poem. **Proofread** your finished poem.
2. Combine your poem with a picture, perhaps coloured with chalk pastels, for an interesting presentation.
3. Make a class display of haiku. Add pictures if you like.
4. Why do you think Sonia Sanchez used unconventional punctuation and capitalization in her poem? Does this add to or detract from the poem's effect?

**CHALLENGE** Find another poem that uses unconventional punctuation and capitalization. Discuss the effect this has on the poem.

Can you figure out the subject of this riddle?

> Although I am usable in the kitchen, I am inedible. As well, I am flexible, movable, and flammable. Some people who cook with me think I am indispensable too. I, being somewhat modest, view myself as simply sensible. What am I?

Did you notice the words that ended in **-able** and **-ible**? The **suffixes -able/-ible** mean "capable of" or "worthy of." Adding the **suffix -able** or **-ible** turns **nouns** and **verbs** into **adjectives**.

## WORD MENU

unthinkable
washable
responsible
horrible
sensible
suitable
enjoyable
reliable
comfortable
variable
believable
terrible
capable
probable
memorable

## Creating Your Word List

**Say these words:**

| suitable | sensible | capable | believable |

What sound do the endings **-able** and **-ible** share? The final unstressed syllable sound "əble" can be spelled **-able** or **-ible**. The symbol ə is an unstressed vowel called a **schwa**.

1.  As a class, make a list of words that end in **-able** and **-ible**. Put the words into a chart like this:

| -able | -ible |
|---|---|
|  |  |

2.  Work with your teacher to create the list of "əble" words you will be learning to spell. You can use: the Word Menu, the riddle, your own words. These are your Lesson Words. Add them to the chart.

**CHALLENGE** Find other words for each chart heading.

### 3. In your notebook
- Write each Lesson Word and circle the letters that make up the "əble" ending.
- Add **-able**, **-ible** words to your Personal Dictionary list.

**STRATEGY SPOT**

## Study Your Spelling Words

**Here are 5 great ways to study your spelling words.**

**1.** "Print" the letters with your finger on your palm.

**2.** Make a missing letter puzzle. For example: **suit _ ble**, **imposs _ ble**.

**3.** Close your eyes and visualize the word in your mind. Open your eyes, write the word, and then check the spelling.

**4.** Highlight the parts of the word you need help remembering.

**5.** Print the word on a strip of paper. Fold the paper like an accordion so each fold contains 1 **syllable**. Spell the word aloud as you unfold each syllable.

**QUICK TIP**

When the **suffix** **-able** or **-ible** is added to some words, the final **silent e** is dropped (lov**e** – lov**able**, sens**e** – sens**ible**). Most "**əble**" words end in **-able**. Guess **-able**, and then **check** in a dictionary.

## Working with Words

**1. Strategy Practice**   Choose 3 Lesson Words you want to practise. Use some of the strategies above to help you learn the spellings.

**2. Word Recognition**   Print a Lesson Word on a card or in your notebook. Use a second card to cover all the letters except the first. Have a partner guess the word. Move the card and show 1 more letter at a time until your partner guesses the word.

**3. Word Sorting**   Write a word that has:
**a)** both a prefix and suffix
**b)** the **long i** sound
**c)** double consonants
**d)** the **long e** sound

**4. Writing Similes**   Write your own words to complete these similes. Use each simile in an interesting sentence.
**a)** as horrible as ...
**b)** as comfortable as ...
**c)** as memorable as ...
**d)** as unthinkable as ...

5. **Incredible Edibles**   Choose items (words and word parts) from each list to make as many 3-course meals (new words) as possible. You can use any word or word part more than once. Check in a dictionary.

| Appetizers | Entrées | Desserts |
|---|---|---|
| re- | desire | -ing |
| un- | touch | -able |
| dis- | use | -ed |
| im- | perfect | -less |
| pre- | mistake | -ful |
| | sent | -ion |
| | think | -en |

**AT HOME**

6. **Describing Words**   Can you find 10 words to describe the various vegetables you might find in your home?

7. **Writing a Word Riddle**   Did you guess the answer to the riddle on page 42? It's a **cookbook**. Write your own riddle using Lesson Words. Exchange riddles with a partner and try to guess each other's answer.

8. **Writing Workshop**   Writers often carry small journals with them to jot down words and sketches of interesting things they see or experience. Start to keep your own Writer's Journal. For the next few days, carry a small notebook or pad with you wherever you go. Jot down memorable things you see or do. You may want to include quick sketches. Use your journal entries to help you write a story or poem.

---

● *DID YOU KNOW?*

The word **inflammable** ("easily set on fire") comes from the Latin *inflammare*. This verb comes from Latin *in-* ("in") and *flamma* ("flame"). Because the **prefix in-** often means "not," to avoid dangerous confusion you will often see the spelling **flammable**.

---

9. **Rearranging Letters**   How many words can you make from the letters found in **indestructible**? You do not need to keep the letters in order. Find at least 25 words. Forty makes you an expert!

# Focus on Language  ADJECTIVES

We can use **adjectives** to describe how something **looks**, **feels**, **sounds**, **tastes**, or **smells**. We can describe a peach as a **round**, **fuzzy**, **edible**, **yellowish-pink** fruit.

**1.** Copy and complete these sentences, using descriptive adjectives:

  **a)** The _____ , _____ meal consisted of _____ roasted corn, _____ potatoes, and fish.

  **b)** The _____ , _____ fish smelled _____ as it cooked over the barbecue coals.

  **c)** The fruit juices were _____ , _____ , and _____ .

**2.** Add adjectives, and then complete the sentences:

  **a)** The _____ , _____ snake slithered across the _____ , _____ grass and ...

  **b)** A _____ , _____ kangaroo leaped ...

**3.** **Writing Workshop**
Reread a story you have read or written recently. Add adjectives to describe the mood, setting, or personality of a character.

**4.** Make a class alphabet for children. Each student chooses a letter and writes a word that begins with it. Add an adjective that begins with the same letter. For example:

angry ape

beautiful baby

Listen to the vowel sounds in this poem.

### The Dream Keeper

Bring me all of your dreams,
You dreamer,
Bring me all your heart melodies
That I may wrap them
In a blue cloud-cloth
Away from the too-rough fingers
Of the world.

— Langston Hughes

### sounded
brought
counting
countries
soup
sought
trouble
though
fought
through
cough
young
dough

# Creating Your Word List

**Say these words:**

• What sound do **ou** and **ough** make in these words?

**shoulder, though**

They make the sound of **long ō**.

• What sound do **ou** and **ough** make in these words?

**cough, fought**

They make the sound of **short ŏ**.

• What sound does **ou** make in these words?

**young, countries, rough**

Did you hear the **short ŭ** sound?

• What sound do **ou** and **ough** make in these words?

**group, through**

Did you hear **long ū** in gr**ou**p and thr**ough**?

1. Make a list of **ou** and **ough** words. The poem will help you. Organize the words by sound, like this:

| long o | short o | long u | short u |
|--------|---------|--------|---------|
|        |         |        |         |

2. Work with your teacher to create the list of **ou** and **ough** words you will be learning to spell. You can use: the Word Menu, the poem, your own words.

3. **In your notebook**
   - Highlight the parts of the words you find difficult.
   - Add **ou** and **ough** words to your Personal Dictionary.

**STRATEGY SPOT**

**Make Wordprints**

Remembering the outline shape of a word can help you recall how to spell it. Notice the differences in these shapes:

soup     fought

# Working with Words

**AT HOME**

1. **Wordprints**   Print your Lesson Words leaving a space between each one. Use a coloured pencil to draw a Wordprint outline around each of your Lesson Words.

2. **Story Ideas**   A dream can give a writer interesting story ideas. Write a story about a dream you have had recently.

3. **Foldover**   Fold a piece of paper like a fan. Make 6 folds. Print a Lesson Word you want to practise on the first fold. Fold over so you can't see the word. On the next fold write the word again. Open up the paper and check your spelling. Repeat practising your word on each fold.

4. **Word Pole**   Copy and complete this Word Pole. When you are done, the letters in the pole will spell the past tense of **to bring**.

a)  a difficult situation
b)  rhymes with **cough**
c)  past tense of **to sound**
d)  used to make bread
e)  antonym of **smooth**
f)  from beginning to end
g)  synonym of **nations**

a) t r o u b l e
b) s o u g h t
c) s o u n d e d
d) d o u g h
e) _ _ _ _ _
f) t h r o u g h
g) _ _ _ _ _ _ _ _

5. **Writing Workshop**   Look at images in the poem at the beginning of the lesson. Look at the phrases used and describe the images that are created. Illustrate one of the images.

**QUICK TIP**

In words like **ou**r and c**ou**nt, you need to pronounce **2** vowel sounds in each word. In these words, **w** is considered a vowel. This sound combination is called a **diphthong**.

6. **Rhyming Words**   A hink-pink is a riddle with a 2-word rhyming answer. For example: What do you call a chubby feline? A **fat cat**. Write the hink-pink answers to these riddles. Each answer word contains **ou**. One word for each answer is in the box.

What do you call …
a) a home for a rodent?
b) twice the difficulty?
c) an earthquake noise?
d) a hefty fish?
e) time for us?
f) people next door's hard work?

| our | stout | trouble |
|---|---|---|
| labour | ground | mouse |

# Focus on Language ▶ DICTIONARY PRONUNCIATIONS

After each word in the dictionary, you will find the word rewritten (in brackets) using **phonetic symbols** (**sim′ bəlz**). Different dictionaries may use different symbols, but the **pronunciation** is the same. This **pronunciation key** helps you in 3 ways by showing: how to pronounce the word, how many syllables it has, and which syllables to stress when you say the word.

1. Find 3 words in the dictionary that you don't know how to say. Use the **pronunciation key** to help you say each word.

---

### Vowel Sounds

| | | | |
|---|---|---|---|
| a | as in **a**nd, b**a**d, s**a**ng | i | as in **i**f, s**i**t, w**i**ll |
| ā | as in f**a**ce, **a**ble, m**ai**l | ī | as in **I**, f**i**ne, b**y** |
| à | as in **a**rt, c**a**r, h**ea**rt | o | as in **o**n, p**o**t, p**aw** |
| e | as in b**e**nd, h**ea**d, wh**e**n | ō | as in r**o**pe, s**oa**p, **ow**n |
| ē | as in b**e**, b**ee**, **ea**t | ò | as in **o**rder, ab**oa**rd, c**o**re |
| ə | as in met**a**l, brok**e**n, penc**i**l, bac**o**n, circ**u**s | u | as in **u**p, **o**ther, s**u**ng |
| | ("ə" is an unstressed vowel called a **schwa**) | ū | as in r**u**de, c**oo**l, bl**ew**, sh**oe** |
| | | ú | as in f**u**ll, c**oo**k, f**u**r, s**ea**rch |

---

2. Write the word that matches each phonetic spelling:
   a) thō       b) sūp       c) sòrs
   d) thrū owt′       e) i nuf′       f) en kùr′ əj mənt

3. **Wound** and **wound** have the same spelling, but different pronunciations and meanings. Write the pronunciation key for each **wound**. Then use each in a sentence.

### FLASHBACK

Can you remember the different sounds of **ou** and **ough**? Think of 1 word to remind you of each sound.

# Spell · Check

## Creating Your Word List

**In your notebook**

- Go to your list of "Words I Still Need to Practise."
- Pick 15 words you need to practise spelling. These are your Review Lesson Words.

## Working with Words

1. **Pronunciation**    Read down your word list, pronouncing each word slowly and clearly.

2. **Highlight**    Where are the trouble spots? Highlight them using a coloured pencil or highlighting pen.

3. **Wordprints**    Draw the Wordprint of each Review Lesson Word. Which words have the same shape?

4. **Identify Prefixes and Suffixes**    Write out any of your words that have a **prefix** or **suffix**. Circle the prefix or suffix.

5. **Visualization**    Use the visualization strategy on page 31 to practise your Review Lesson Words.

6. **Word Explosion**    "Explode" the words below by adding **prefixes** and **suffixes**. Write as many new words as you can. You will need to make changes to some of the words before adding word parts. Check in a dictionary.
   **a)** think          **b)** view          **c)** suit          **d)** please

7. **Letter Patterns**    Write **ent** on 1 sheet of paper and **ough** on another. Each partner has a sheet of paper and in 2 minutes writes as many words as possible that contain these letter patterns. Score 1 point for each correctly spelled word.

**AT HOME**

8. **Practise Your Spelling Words**    Look back at the Strategy Spot on page 43. Use some of the ideas to study your Review Lesson Words at home.

9. **Word Meanings**   Play "I'm Thinking of a Lesson Word" with a partner. Pick a Lesson Word. Give your partner a clue about the word one clue at a time. (Be careful not to say the word!) See if your partner can guess the word in 3 tries.

10. **Word Stairs**   Write down a Lesson Word. Use the last letter of the word to start the next word. How far down can you make the stairs go? Do it like this:

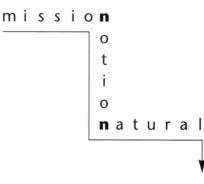

**Proofreading Spotlight**

## COPS

**COPS** is an acronym that stands for: **C**apitals, **O**rganization, **P**unctuation, **S**pelling. Use COPS in proofreading your work. When you check organization, think about **(a)** word order in each sentence and **(b)** sentence order in each paragraph. Each COPS item is a separate step. Check capitals first, and then go back and check organization. Checking punctuation is the next step, and spelling the last.

*Proofread one of your stories or reports using COPS. Remember to proofread each item as a separate step!*

## FLASHBACK

Cross off your list the Review Lesson Words you now know how to spell. Which spelling strategies work best for you? Make a note of these and use them often!

6. **Word Web**   Pick 1 of your Lesson Words. What 2 words does it make you think of? What other words does each new word make you think of? Add as many words as you can to make a Word Web.

   CHALLENGE   Use your web as the basis for a story or poem you write in class or at home.

● **DID YOU KNOW?**

The **prefixes il-, im-,** and **ir-** are all variations of the **prefix in-**. We add **il-** before the letter **l, ir-** before **r,** and **im-** before **b, m,** or **p.**

7. **Writing Workshop**   Some of the best story ideas can start from a picture. Draw a picture and write a story based on your illustration.

8. **Concentration**   Cut a sheet of paper into 20 equal-sized squares. Write your Lesson Words twice — 1 word per square. Turn the squares over, and then mix them up. Number the **back** of the squares from 1 to 20. Lay the squares down so that the numbers are showing. Take turns turning over 2 numbers until you get a pair of matching words.

9. **Adding mis-**   Add the **prefix mis-** to each of these words. Then write a short defining sentence. For example: behave – **mis**behave. **Misbehave** means to behave badly.

   a) spell       b) pronounce       c) fortune       d) understand

10. **Synonyms**   Work with a partner. Try to write at least 1 **synonym** (similar meaning) for each of your Lesson Words. Use a thesaurus or dictionary if you need help.

FLASHBACK

What are some of the ways our study of prefixes, suffixes, and root words has helped you become a better speller?

# Connecting with TECHNOLOGY

### The World Wide Web

The **World Wide Web** is a service of the Internet (**Inter**national **Net**work linking computers). At each site on the web, you see a page of text and pictures on the screen. By clicking on words that are highlighted and underlined, your computer is automatically <u>linked</u> to another place on the Internet. To view web pages and follow their links, you use a program called a **web browser**, such as Netscape Navigator™ or Microsoft Internet Explorer™. Here is the first (**home**) page of Nelson Canada's web site: ● ● ● ● ● ● ● ● ● ● ● ● ● ●➤

**Y**ou can go directly to a web page if you know its address. Each address is a series of letters, figures, dots, and words called an **URL** (Uniform **R**esource **L**ocator). You don't need to know what the parts of an URL mean, but you DO have to copy them into the web browser EXACTLY (no capital letters or spaces)! Here is the URL for Nelson Canada's home page:

⇨ http://zelda.thomson.com/nelson.html

1. Design a web page to tell about YOU. What pictures would you use? What would you write? Web pages often show short videos and play sounds. What moving pictures and sounds would you add? What links to other places would you provide?
2. Create the web page on paper, with your own text and pictures or words and photos from magazines. You can also use a computer to design your page. Use your spelling strategies to practise interesting words. **Proofread** your final version, and create a class display.

Read each **rebus** sentence, substituting a word for the picture.

Be sure to  me before you arrive. I'll meet you at the

+way. We'll go to the office where Mom works.

She's a super+ at the tele+ station. She'll

be happy to help us with our technology project.

## WORD MENU

submarine

subway

subtitle

submerge

television

telephone

telescope

telecast

telecommunication

superhuman

supervision

supermarket

superior

## Creating Your Word List

**Say these words:**

- Say the word created when the **prefix tele-** is added to:

### phone, graph, vision

The **prefix tele-** means "over a distance" (**tele**communication — communication over a distance).

- Say the word created when the **prefix sub-** is added to:

### way, merge, divide

The **prefix sub-** usually means "below" or "under" (**sub**way — underground way, **sub**zero — below zero degrees).

- Say the word created when the **prefix super-** is added to:

### star, market, vision

The **prefix super-** can mean "great," "above," or "more." For example, **super**human.

**1.** Make a list of words that use these prefixes.

**2.** Work with your teacher to create the list of **tele-**, **sub-**, and **super-** Lesson Words you will be learning to spell. You can use: the Word Menu, the rebus, your own words.

### 3. In your notebook
- Write the Lesson Words and highlight the **prefixes**.
- You may want to add **tele-**, **sub-**, and **super-** words to your Personal Dictionary. Be sure to keep it up to date.

**STRATEGY SPOT**

## Look for Word Origins (Etymology)

Ancient Greek and Latin have given us many prefixes, suffixes, and words. If you link words with the same origin, you may find that they share spelling patterns.

# Working with Words

**1. Word Definitions**  Look back at the meanings of the **prefixes tele-**, **sub-**, and **super-**. Use them to help you write definitions for each word below. For example: **subtitle** — a title or line of words below a picture.
a) submarine  b) subhead  c) subtropical
d) substandard  e) television  f) telephoto lens
g) superhuman  h) supermarket  i) superstar

**2. Illustrating Prefixes**  Draw pictures to illustrate the meaning of 3 of your Lesson Words — one that starts with **sub-**, one with **tele-**, and one with **super-**. How does the prefix affect the meaning of the word?

**3. Word Origins**  Match each food word to its original language. You can use a dictionary if you need help with any words.

| Algonkian | Spanish | Ukrainian | Yiddish |
|-----------|---------|-----------|---------|
| Italian | French | Chinese | Arabic |

a) spaghetti  b) tortilla  c) croissant  d) squash
e) tea  f) perogy  g) bagel  h) falafel

**AT HOME**

**4. Describing a Television Program**  Watch a television program at home, and then write a short description of it.

**5. Word Meanings**   Copy and complete this Word Pole. Use the clues to write Word Menu words. The letters in the circles name housing areas just outside cities.

**a)** this enlarges distant objects
**b)** excellent
**c)** a large underwater vessel
**d)** the overseeing of others
**e)** a place to buy groceries
**f)** go beneath the surface
**g)** a television broadcast

a) _ _ _ _ ⊘ _ _ _ _
b) _ ⊘ _ _ _ _ _ _ _
c) _ _ ⊘ _ _ _ _ _ _
d) _ ⊘ _ _ _ _ _ _ _ _ _ _ _
e) _ _ _ _ ⊘ _ _ _ _ _ _
f) _ _ ⊘ _ _ _ _ _
g) _ _ _ _ _ _ ⊘ _

**6. Word Web**   Write a Lesson Word. What 2 words does it make you think of? Add as many other words as you can to make a Word Web. Use your web as the basis for a story or poem.

## ● DID YOU KNOW ?

Many words come to us from Latin and Greek with prefixes already attached. That's why there is no English root for words like **subtract**.

**7. Writing Workshop**   Some of your Word Menu words may give you story ideas. For example, **superhuman** could be in an adventure story, **telecommunication** could relate to the invention of a system that reads minds, and **submarine** could describe a new way of travel under the sea. Use the Word Menu to help you come up with story ideas in your next writing class.

### FLASHBACK

Look back at the lessons you have done so far. List 3 ways that words are formed.

# Connecting with MATH

## Geometric Shape Names

Naming geometric shapes is easy if you think about how our language works.

**1.** Look up the meanings of these prefixes:
   **a)** uni-
   **b)** bi-
   **c)** tri-
   **d)** quadri-/quadr-
   **e)** oct-/octo-/octa-
   **f)** sept-
   **g)** deca-/dec-
   **h)** centi-
   **i)** poly-

**2.** Write 2 words that begin with each prefix. Check the spellings in a dictionary. Use your spelling strategies to practise them.

**3.** Write the name of each of these shapes:

   **a)**    **b)**    **c)**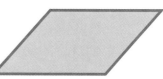

**4.** **Math Trivia** Test your math and language skills knowledge:
   **a)** Create a **mnemonic device** to help you remember that a hexagon has 6 sides.
   **b)** What is special about the Pentagon building in Washington, DC?
   **c)** How many limbs does an octopus have?
   **d)** What is a tripod?
   **e)** What is a quadrangle?
   **f)** What are quintuplets?
   **g)** What is an octogenarian?
   **h)** How many performers are in a trio? a quartet?
   **i)** What does **bilingual** mean?

   **CHALLENGE**   Can you draw a **nonagon**?

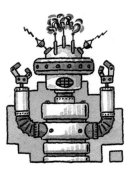

Can you discover the common action the android is being taught?

### Commands for an Android

1. Open door and carefully remove object from cupboard.
2. Turn handle slowly clockwise to open.
3. Place object directly under flow.
4. Fill object.
5. Turn handle quickly counterclockwise to close.
6. Lift object carefully to mouth and dispose of contents.

## WORD MENU

nearly

carefully

happily

luckily

really

mostly

quickly

completely

finally

usually

lately

quietly

lovely

friendly

colourfully

# Creating Your Word List

### Say these words:

| near | nearly | happy | happily |

What sound is made by the **-ly** ending? Notice what happens to the **y** in happ**y** – happ**i**ly. The **suffix -ly** is added to many adjectives to turn them into adverbs. For example: It is a **quick** squirrel. The squirrel climbs **quickly**. **Quick** is an adjective and **quickly** is an adverb.

**1.** Make a list of words that end in the **suffix -ly**.

**2.** Work with your teacher to create the list of **-ly** words you will be learning to spell. You can use: the Word Menu, the android commands, your own words.

**3. In your notebook**
- Write the Lesson Words and circle each **suffix -ly**.
- Add **-ly** words to your Personal Dictionary.
- Did you figure out that the android was being taught how to pour and drink a glass of water?

**CHALLENGE** Choose a common action and write your own android commands. Have a partner act out the commands to guess your action.

## Find Hands-on Strategies That Work!

Some words require extra practice. Try writing them in sand or on a chalkboard. Model these words in clay. Draw a circle or square and fill it up by writing the word over and over.

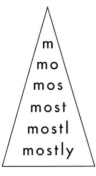

```
m
mo
mos
most
mostl
mostly
```

# Working with Words

1. **Word Pyramid**   Choose a Lesson Word that you need to practise. Draw a triangle. On the first line, print the first letter of the word. On the second line, print the first 2 letters. Continue until the triangle is full. Build a word pyramid with 5 other Lesson Words.

2. **Alphabetizing**   Write your Lesson Words in alphabetical order.

3. **Word Meanings**   Write the **Across** and **Down** clues that go with each word in this crossword puzzle.

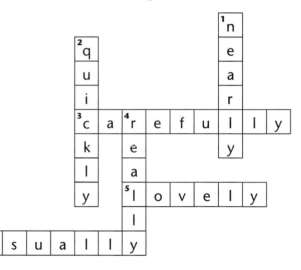

*colourfully*

## QUICK TIP

A good rule is to add just **-ly** unless the word would look strange. Then you only need to know that when a word ends in **-ic**, you add **-ally** (basic – basically).

4. **Charting Actions**   Complete this chart in your notebook to tell what you do carefully, quickly, happily, and quietly.

| carefully | quickly | happily | quietly |
|-----------|---------|---------|---------|
|           |         |         |         |

**5.** **Adding -ly**   Sometimes you need to make changes in a word before adding the **suffix -ly**. For example:

late – lately      capable – capably      lucky – luckily

Add **-ly** to each of the words below and write the new word.
a) hasty      b) near      c) gentle      d) careful
e) colourful      f) lucky      g) real      h) private

**AT HOME**

**6.** **Practise Difficult Words**   Look through your Personal Dictionary list. Which words are still difficult to spell? Use ideas from the Strategy Spot on page 61 to practise them.

**7.** **Completing Sentences**   Complete these sentence beginnings:
a) I nearly always ...      b) I usually find that ...
c) Lately, I have ...      d) Finally, I ...

**8.** **Adding Adverbs to Verbs**   Play this game with a partner. Think of a verb (**sing**). Write down 3 adverbs that could describe it (**loudly**, **softly**, **sweetly**). Tell your first adverb to your partner. If she or he can't guess your verb, then say the second adverb, and so on. Switch roles and play again.

**9.** **Writing Workshop**   Instructions are another form of writing. Look at the **Commands for an Android** at the beginning of the lesson. Write your own set of instructions. See if a classmate can tell what you have described.

**10.** **Timely Words**   The adverb **daily** means "each day." Write what each of these words means:
a) weekly      b) monthly      c) annually

For each word, name something that happens during that time. For example: **daily** — sunrises.

**11.** **Adjectives to Adverbs**   When **-ly** is added to an adjective, the new word is usually an adverb. Rewrite the following sentences, changing the adjectives into adverbs:

The excited fans cheered.
The quick girl leaped over the ditch.

# Focus on Language  ADVERBS

A **noun** is a person, place, thing, or emotion.
An **adjective** describes a noun.
A **verb** is an action or state of being.
An **adverb** describes a verb.

An adverb can answer the questions **how? when?** or **where?**

> Alison read **quietly** in the library. (**how**)
> She had arrived **early** to find a good seat. (**when**)
> I am going to meet her **there**. (**where**)

1. Rewrite these sentences, adding descriptive **adverbs**:
   a) The snake slithered. (**how**?)
   b) The bisons stampeded. (**when**?)
   c) The lion went. (**where**?)

2. Use parts of speech and pictures to create an **ANVA** poem. Write an Adjective, a Noun, a Verb, and then an Adverb.

3. Rewrite this paragraph adding adverbs to make the story more interesting.

   > Maria went to her room to check up on her snake. As she walked toward the terrarium, she noticed the lid was off. She looked all around her room. Then she saw it! Before she reached the snake, it slithered out of the room — to the horror of her father.

   **CHALLENGE**   Write another paragraph to complete the story.

> **FLASHBACK**
>
> How can you remember to use adverbs in your story writing?

If you were Alex, would you respond to this e-mail message?

> Alex: I'm in desperate trouble! Julius has disappeared. The private eye I hired to find him has had no luck. Julius's health is so delicate — I've been so protective of him. His size will be an advantage. And we all know how fond of garbage he is, so he won't go hungry. I must have courage. Do you have any tips that will help me find him?

What word endings can you find in the message?

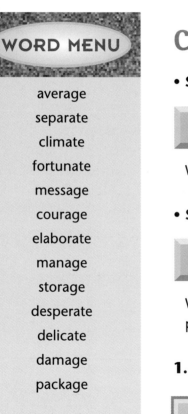

**WORD MENU**

average

separate

climate

fortunate

message

courage

elaborate

manage

storage

desperate

delicate

damage

package

## Creating Your Word List

• **Say these words:**

| average | manage | package |
|---------|--------|---------|

What sound does the ending **-age** make?

• **Say these words:**

| desperate | delicate | separate |
|-----------|----------|----------|

What sound does the ending **-ate** make? Do you know another pronunciation for the **-ate** ending in **separate**?

1.  Make a list of **-age** and **-ate** words. Put them into a chart like this:

| -age | -ate |
|------|------|
|      |      |

2.  Work with your teacher to create the list of **-age** and **-ate** Lesson Words you will be learning to spell. You can use: the Word Menu, the e-mail message, your own words.

**3. In your notebook**
- Write each Lesson Word and underline the part that you need to practise.
- Add **-age** and **-ate** words to your Personal Dictionary. Use them in your reading and writing.

### Look for Word Families

Make letter pattern links between words you know how to spell and those you are learning. If you can spell pack**age**, then you can also spell advant**age**.

# Working with Words

**QUICK TIP**

Usually you just add **-age** to a word. Here are the exceptions:
- Change final **y** to **i**: marry – marr**iage**.
- Double final letter in short-vowel words: cot – cot**tage**.
- Drop final **e**: dose – dos**age**.

**1. At a Mighty Rate** Draw a line down the centre of a page in your notebook. Write **ight** at the top of 1 column, and **ate** at the top of the other column. In 3 minutes, write as many words as you can that contain these patterns. Check in your dictionary. Score 1 point for each correctly spelled word. Subtract 1 point for any spelling that is not a real word. Have fun!

**CHALLENGE** Use 3 of your words in interesting sentences.

**2. -ate Word Analogies** Write an **-ate** word to complete each analogy in your notebook:
- a) **fear** is to **afraid** as **despair** is to _____.
- b) **simple** is to _____ as **easy** is to **difficult**.
- c) **strong** is to **durable** as **fragile** is to _____.
- d) **open** is to **close** as _____ is to **join**.
- e) **good** is to **bad** as _____ is to **unlucky**.

**CHALLENGE** Write 3 of your own **-ate** word analogies to share.

**3. Adding Vowels** Complete the following Lesson Words in your notebook, filling in the blanks with the correct **vowels**.
- a) d _ sp _ r _ t _
- b) c _ _ r _ g _
- c) s _ p _ r _ t _
- d) cl _ m _ t _
- e) g _ rb _ g _
- f) _ v _ r _ g _

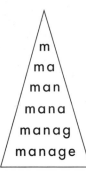

m
ma
man
mana
manag
manage

**4. Word Pyramid**  Build word pyramids with 5 Lesson Words. Draw a triangle. At the top, print the first letter of the word. On the second line, print the first 2 letters. On the third line, print the first 3 letters. Continue until the triangle is full.

**5. Suffix -age Meanings**  The **suffix -age** can have several meanings:
- result of, as in **breakage**
- rate of, as in **dosage**
- fee or charge, as in **postage**
- action or process, as in **haulage**

Add **-age** to these words and sort them by suffix meaning.

| | | | |
|---|---|---|---|
| **a)** carry | **b)** wreck | **c)** block | **d)** use |
| **e)** marry | **f)** link | **g)** pack | **h)** store |

**CHALLENGE**  Use 3 of the new words in a paragraph or poem.

**6. Garage Sale**  Make a list of items you and your family would sell at a garage sale and price them.

AT HOME

● *DID YOU KNOW?*

**Garage** comes from the French word **garer**, "to guard."

**7. Writing Workshop**  When you are writing, you use different styles depending on your audience. Compare the style in this book with the style you use in story writing. Make a list of the differences.

**8. Memory Game**  Play this game in a group. Player A says "I went on a trip and took an ... (something that begins with **a**)." Player B says "I went on a trip and took an ... (repeat the **a** item) and a ... (add something that begins with **b**)." Keep taking turns repeating all the items before adding a new one. Can you make it to **z**?

FLASHBACK

Do any of the words in your Personal Dictionary have a common letter pattern? Can you make a link between one of these words and one you know?

## Family Lineage

Families are very interesting. It is fun to explore all the family connections in your family tree. You can trace your own **lineage** back to your ancestors. The word **lineage** (lin′ ē ij′) can mean "direct descent from a particular ancestor" or "the descendants of a common ancestor."

1. Explore your own family tree. Use a Family Web like the one below.
2. Your Family Web may soon grow quite large. Use a big piece of paper, or one sheet for each branch of your tree. Start at the **bottom** of the page.
3. Talk to your family members and relatives to get as much information as you can.
4. What is unusual about the spelling of **lineage**? Why do you think the final **e** was NOT dropped when adding **-age**? The pronunciation of the word will give you a clue.

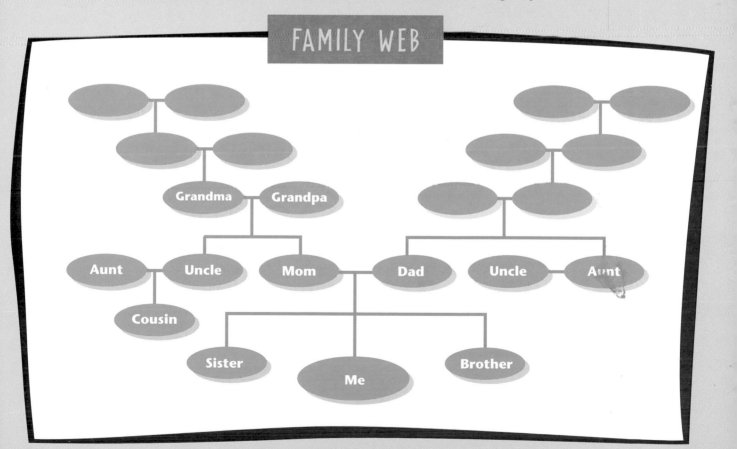

FAMILY WEB

What vowel sound does the pattern **ow** make in this limerick?

> The cautious collapsible cow
> Gives milk by the sweat of her brow;
>     Then under the trees
>     She folds her front knees
> And sinks fore and aft with a bow.

> — Arthur Guiterman

## WORD MENU

follow

powerful

window

frown

bowl

below

crowd

lowering

scowl

throwing

towel

pillow

shadow

township

owning

# Creating Your Word List

• **Say these words:**

| scowl | towel | crowd |

What sound does the pattern **ow** make in these words? This sound combination is called a **diphthong**. In a diphthong, you pronounce **2** vowel sounds in each word. In these words, **w** is considered a **vowel**.

• **Say these words:**

| bowl | window | pillow |

What sound does **ow** make in these words? It makes the sound of **long o**.

**1.** Make a list of **ow** words. The limerick will help you. Organize the words by sound, for example:

| long o | diphthong |
|--------|-----------|
|        |           |
|        |           |

**2.** Work with your teacher to create the list of **ow** words you will be learning to spell. You can use: the Word Menu, the limerick, your own words. These are your Lesson Words.

**3. In your notebook**
- Write the Lesson Words and <u>underline</u> **ow** in each word.
- You may want to add **ow** words to your Personal Dictionary.
- The limerick contained the words **fore** and **aft**. What do they mean? What compound words are they found in?

STRATEGY SPOT

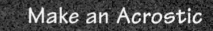

## Make an Acrostic

You need to pay close attention to short words that are spelled alike or have a spelling you can't sound out. Using the letters of the word to make up an **acrostic** helps you remember the order of the letters. Here is how you do it:

**1.** Print the word in a column.

**2.** Write a word for each letter. It helps if the words make a sentence. For example:
The
**H**og
**E**ats
**N**ow

**3.** Pick a Lesson Word that is challenging for you and try out this spelling strategy.

**4.** Read a partner's acrostic.

**5.** `CHALLENGE` Write an acrostic poem in which each letter begins a verse rather than a single word.

# Working with Words

**1. Strategy Practice**  Choose another Lesson Word you want to practise. Use its letters to write an acrostic sentence.

**2. Homophones**  **Homophones** sound the same but are spelled differently and have different meanings. Write a brief definition or draw a small picture for each homophone:
   a) foul/fowl        b) bough/bow        c) flour/flower
   d) groan/grown      e) road/rode        f) toad/towed

`CHALLENGE`  Use each of the homophone pairs in a sentence. For example: **threw/through** — Ramona **threw** the ball **through** the hoop.

**3.** **Writing Workshop**   Some Word Menu words create strong images for readers: **powerful**, **shadow**, **scowl**. What other words inspire a strong response from readers? Read over the stories in your writing folder and look for words that can be replaced with words that create strong images.

**4.** **Word Associations**   Play a Word Association game with a partner. Say a Lesson Word (for example, **yellow**). Your partner responds with a word that goes with your word. Take turns until you cannot think of any other words.

## QUICK TIP

The **diphthong "ow"** can also be spelled **ou** (ouch, loud) and **ough** (bough, slough).

● **DID YOU KNOW ?**
Our word **frown** comes from the Old French word *froigner*, which means "to turn up one's nose." Do **you** turn up your nose when you frown?

**5.** **Adding Vowels**   The vowels have been removed from the following groups of letters. Return them to make **ow** words. Remember that **w** is considered a **vowel** in **ow diphthongs**!

  **a)** wnd      **b)** pllw      **c)** cln      **d)** thrng
  **e)** lwr      **f)** crdd      **g)** blw      **h)** tnshp

  **CHALLENGE**   These groups of letters are missing vowels **and** the letters have been mixed up. Rewrite each word.

  **i)** hwds      **j)** rp      **k)** gnw      **l)** wsghn

**6.** **Make a Collage**   Make an **ow** collage. Use words and pictures that contain **ow**. For example, you can include yell**ow** paper, a picture of a cl**ow**n, and the words **flower** and **tower**.

**AT HOME**

**7.** **Finding ow Words**   Find all the **ow** words hidden around your house. Look in all the rooms — and don't forget to look in drawers and cupboards too!

**FLASHBACK**

What are 3 good spelling habits you have acquired? How do they help you spell new words?

## Limericks

A limerick is a short, humorous poem. Most are fanciful — they do not make much sense — but all limericks have the same structure.

1. Reread the limerick on page 68 that began this lesson. Look at its structure — number of lines, rhyming words, and line lengths. List your findings.

2. Read the limerick below. Add to your list any other information you learn about writing a limerick.

> The limerick's lively to write:
> Five lines to it — all nice and tight.
> Two long ones, two trick
> Little short ones; then quick
> As a flash here's the last one in sight.
>
> — David McCord

3. Using your list as a guide, write a limerick on a topic of your choice. When you are finished, check that you have made no structure errors (for example, too many lines). Then **proofread** using the COPS outline on page 51.

4. Make any changes, and copy your limerick on a large piece of paper. You can decorate it by drawing or painting items you included in your limerick.

   **CHALLENGE** Write another limerick. This time, include **ow** words. You're a word magician if you can use words with BOTH **ow** sounds in your limerick!

5. Look in the library for the limericks of **Edward Lear** (British, 1812-1888). If you have a computer with a web browser, you'll find a selection of his poetry and art at the Italian web site below. (See page 55 for information on the World Wide Web.)

http://www2.pair.com/mgraz/Lear/index.html

# Spell · Check

## Creating Your Word List

**In your notebook**

• Go to your list of "Words I Still Need to Practise."
• Pick 15 words you need to practise spelling. These are your Review Lesson Words.

## Working with Words

1. **Exaggerate Pronunciation**   Read your words. Exaggerate the pronunciation of silent letters or odd letter patterns.

2. **Prefixes**   Write words in groups that share a common prefix. What does the prefix mean?

3. **Rhyming Words**   Beside each word on the list write a rhyming word that shares a common letter pattern.

4. **Letter Patterns**   Knock over the bowling pins by writing 5 words for each letter pattern.

5. **Recognizing Spellings**   Pick the correct spelling in each row. Then use each word in an interesting sentence.
   a) telephone          teliphone          telefone
   b) carefily           carefuly           carefully
   c) iresponsible       irresponsible      unresponsible

**6. Synonyms** Write a synonym for each of these words:

    **a)** owning      **b)** detective      **c)** lovely      **d)** unhappiness

    **e)** below      **f)** average      **g)** delicate      **h)** misfortune

**AT HOME**

**7. Practise Your Spelling Words** Look back at the Strategy Spot on page 43. Use some of the ideas to study your Review Lesson Words at home.

**8. Word Chain** See how long a word chain you can make. Write down a Review Lesson Word. Use the last letter of that word to start the next word. For example:

    unfamilia(**r**      **r**)elat(**e**      **e**)ffectiv**e**

*Proofreading Spotlight*

## Read Aloud

After you have finished writing a story, try reading it aloud to yourself. Your ears will pick up on things your eyes miss on their own:

- Your voice will stop at the end of a sentence — Did you use a period?
- Your voice will rise if you ask a question — Did you use a question mark?
- Are you changing your voice because people are talking? — Did you use quotation marks?
- Did you leave a word out?
- Did you write a word twice?

*Look back at an unedited piece of writing. Check it by reading aloud.*

You can also revise your writing by reading it aloud to a partner.

*Practise your oral fluency by reading a book to a kindergarten class. You'll have to read with enthusiasm to keep the children's interest!*

### FLASHBACK

Look at the Review Lesson Words you now know how to spell. Cross them off your list of "Words I Still Need to Practise." Bravo! You're becoming a spelling superstar.

Look at this dictionary definition.

> **contraction** (kən trak′ shən) *n.* a shortened form of two words: ***Isn't*** *is a contraction of* ***is not***.

What other contractions do you know?

**WORD MENU**

I'd
that's
we'd
shouldn't
doesn't
didn't
couldn't
wouldn't
weren't
hadn't
they'll
they're

## Creating Your Word List

**1.** Look at these words and their **contractions**:

should not – shouldn't    had not – hadn't    they will – they'll

What happens when you form each contraction? Most contractions follow the same pattern: a vowel in the second word is removed and replaced by an apostrophe ('). Which contraction does not follow this pattern?

**2.** What words form these **contractions**?

I'd    we'd    she'd

What happened when these contractions were formed? Record the letters that were dropped in the contractions.

**3.** As a class, make a list of **contractions**.

**4.** Work with your teacher to create the list of **contractions** you will be learning to spell. You can use: the Word Menu, the definition, your own words. Include these 2 **challenge words** in your Lesson Words:

**it's, you're**

**5. In your notebook**
- Write each Lesson Word, and beside it write the words from which the contraction was formed.
- Keep adding **contractions** to your Personal Dictionary. Keep the list up to date to help in your writing.

## Identify Words in a Contraction

Look at this sentence: **We'd like to have gone.** You know that the contraction is made up of the words **we would** because **we had** would not make sense in the sentence.

# Working with Words

couldnot

couldn't

1. **Forming Contractions** On a strip of paper, write the 2 words that form each Lesson Word. Do NOT leave a space between the words. Fold the paper to cover the letter, or letters, that are replaced by the apostrophe. Staple the paper vertically to hold the fold in place. The staple shows where the apostrophe goes in the contraction.

2. **Charting Contractions** Copy and complete this chart. The first line has been done for you.

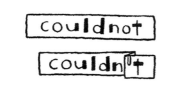

QUICK TIP

| Pronoun | + am/ are/is | + will | + would | + has/ have | + had |
|---------|-------------|--------|---------|-------------|-------|
| I | I'm | I'll | I'd | I've | I'd |
| you | a) | b) | c) | d) | e) |
| she | f) | g) | h) | i) | j) |
| he | k) | l) | m) | n) | o) |
| we | p) | q) | r) | s) | t) |
| they | u) | v) | w) | x) | y) |

**CHALLENGE** Use 1 contraction from each column in an interesting sentence.

Many writers confuse **its** and **it's**. **Its** (no apostrophe) is an adjective: The cat drank **its** milk. **It's** (with an apostrophe) is a contraction for **it is**: **It's** cold today.

3. **Shortening Words** We also shorten our speech by leaving off parts of a word. Write the short forms for these words:
   a) submarine      b) chimpanzee      c) physical education
   d) telephone      e) gymnasium       f) veterinarian
   g) rhinoceros     h) electronic mail i) photograph

4. **Matching Contraction Words** Play this game with a partner. Write the following words on cards:

| that | were | have | can | could | not | are | we | has |
|------|------|------|-----|-------|-----|-----|----|-----|
| is | would | she | it | us | let | they | I | am |

Shuffle the cards and place them facedown. Turn over 2 cards. If possible, make a contraction from the words on the cards and write it down on a piece of paper. Pick up the cards, shuffle them, and place them facedown for your partner, who repeats the activity. Take turns. The player with the most contractions written down wins!

### ● DID YOU KNOW ?
The root of the word **contraction** is the verb **contract**, meaning "to become smaller" or "to shrink."

5. **Contractions in Writing** Look through a book you are reading. Find a paragraph that contains contractions (pages with dialogue would be a good place to start) and one that does not (you may have to look in another book). Which paragraph sounds more formal? How might an author decide whether to use contractions?

6. **Writing Workshop** Sometimes contractions are used in titles and headlines. Write some story titles with and without contractions. Which works better? Why?

7. **Matching Homophones** Work with a partner to find **homophone pairs** that include contractions (for example: **they're/there**). For each, write the contraction on one piece of paper and a sentence using its homophone on another. Trade papers with another pair of students and match each sentence to its homophone contraction.

**AT HOME**

8. **Media Search** Find 3 advertisements that use contractions (newspaper, magazine, TV, radio). For each ad, list the product advertised, type (illustration, photograph, "interview," animation), and form of language used (slang, formal, informal, and so on). Was the advertisement successful? Why or why not?

# Focus on Language  POSSESSIVES

Apostrophes are also used to show ownership. For example, instead of saying **the hat of the boy**, we say **the boy's hat**. Both phrases mean the same — the boy owns (possesses) the hat.

**1.** The **possessive form** of a singular noun is made by adding an apostrophe plus **-s**. Rewrite these phrases, using possessives:

   **a)** the yard of the cat       **b)** the collar of the dog

   **c)** the cheese of the mouse    **d)** the jacket of Rashid

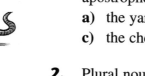

**2.** Plural nouns like the ones below are changed to their possessive form in the same way: children – children**'s**. Rewrite these phrases, using possessive forms:

   **a)** the coats of the women    **b)** the hats of the men

   **c)** the homes of the people    **d)** the honks of the geese

**3.** Plural nouns ending in **-s** are changed to their possessive form by adding only an apostrophe, dogs – dogs**'**. Rewrite these phrases, using possessive forms:

   **a)** the team of the girls      **b)** the baseball of the boys

   **c)** the feathers of the birds    **d)** the car of the Chens

**4.** Pronouns form the possessive in special ways:

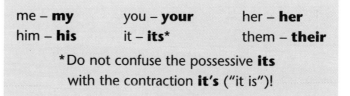

| me – **my** | you – **your** | her – **her** |
|---|---|---|
| him – **his** | it – **its*** | them – **their** |

*Do not confuse the possessive **its** with the contraction **it's** ("it is")!

Rewrite these phrases, using possessive forms:

   **a)** the notebook of me     **b)** the name of she

   **c)** the number of it       **d)** the address of them

**FLASHBACK**

How can what you've learned about using apostrophes in contractions and possessives help you as a writer?

Would you attend this auction if you could?

**PUBLIC AUCTION — August 14, 1997**

1. Brand-new automobile parts ('67 Chevrolet)
2. Tasteful lawn ornaments (glow-in-the-dark gnomes)
3. Comfortable straw bed (no lumps)
4. Slightly mauled animal carrier (lion-sized)
5. Genuine autographs (including Elvis)
6. Barely used saw (for trimming telephone poles)

**Auctioneer: I.M. Authentic**

## WORD MENU

applaud
auction
August
author
automobile
audience
taught
lawn
yawn
fawn
awful
caught
caution
daughter
crawling

# Creating Your Word List

**Say these words:**

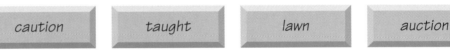

| caution | taught | lawn | auction |

What **vowel sound** do these 4 words have in common? Which letter patterns make the **short o** sound in these words?

**1.** Make a list of **au**, **augh**, and **aw** words. Chart the words:

| au | augh | aw |
|----|------|----|
|    |      |    |

**2.** Work with your teacher to create the list of **au**, **augh**, and **aw** words you will be learning to spell. You can use: the Word Menu, the auction notice, your own words.

**3. In your notebook**
- Write the Lesson Words and underline the **short o** sound.
- Add **au**, **augh**, and **aw** words to your Personal Dictionary.

## Doodle Your Words!

Doodling is a great way to practise your spelling words! After a pretest, take small pieces of paper and on each one correctly spell a word. Then fill the sheet by doodling the word in different letter styles, sizes, and colours.

# Working with Words

1. **Strategy Practice**   Use doodling to practise 3 Lesson Words.

2. **Adding Spelling Patterns**   Reorganize the letters and add **au** or **aw** to spell a Word Menu word. For example: ghtt + **au** = **taught**.
   a) roth
   b) fn
   c) yn
   d) boomtile
   e) gcth
   f) luf
   g) ln
   h) pdlpa

3. **Writing Synonyms**   Write 5 synonyms for the word **awesome**. Reread some of the stories in your writing folder. Where could you use a synonym for **awesome**?

4. **Prefix auto- Meanings**   The **prefix auto-** means "self," "same," or "automatic." Write a definition for each word.
   a) autograph
   b) automobile
   c) autobiography
   d) autopilot
   e) automotive
   f) autodestruct

   **CHALLENGE**   Illustrate 2 of these words.

5. **Write an Auction Notice**   What could you clear out of your classroom or home to auction off? Write up your own auction list like the one on page 78.

6. **Word Explosion**   Watch the word **applaud** "explode"!

applauding   applaud   applauds   applauded

Explode the words below by adding **-s**, **-ed**, **-ing**, or **-er**. Write as many new words as you can. You may need to use a dictionary to make sure each new word makes sense.
   a) yawn
   b) crawl
   c) caution

**QUICK TIP**

Other patterns that make the **short o** sound are **ou** (cough), **ah** (Utah), **oa** (broad), and **ach** (yacht). The **au** pattern can also have the sound of **short a** (laugh).

**7. Writing Workshop**   Often, novels have a short biography of the author on the back cover or inside the book. Work on your own biography (autobiography) to include at the end of your next story.

**8. I'm Thinking of ...**   Play "I'm Thinking of a Lesson Word" with a partner. Pick a Lesson Word. Give your partner a clue about the word. See if your partner can guess the word in 3 tries.

**CHALLENGE**   Pick 4 Lesson Words and write a sentence for each word. Share your sentences with a partner.

---

● *DID YOU KNOW?*

New words are always coming into our vocabulary. Here are some words and the years when they were coined: **fax** (1948), **VCR** (1971), **junkfood** (1975), **cyberspace** (1984).

---

**9. Word Trip**   Copy the boxes and follow the arrows. Write a word you think of when you say the word you just left. Add and fill in 3 more boxes.

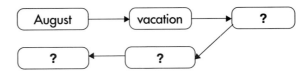

August → vacation → ?
? ← ? ←

Make 3 of your own word trips. Start with Lesson Words and make each word trip at least 7 words long.

**CHALLENGE**   Use a Word Trip to write a story or poem.

AT HOME

**10. Sentence Completions**   Complete these sentences at home. See how many **au**, **augh**, and **aw** words you can use!
   **a)** August is an awesome month because …
   **b)** The audience applauded when …
   **c)** The snake crawled …

FLASHBACK

Are you a doodler? If so, when do you doodle?

## Advertising Travel

Have you heard or seen tourism slogans? Tourism agencies use slogans on radio and TV to entice the audience to book a trip to their city, province, or country. For example:

1. Write a travel slogan for your community, province, territory, or country. It should encourage others to want to come visit.

2. Now write a slogan for a place in the world YOU would like to visit, real or imagined. If you have a computer with a web browser, you'll find tourist information links for 150 countries and all the provinces of Canada and states of the USA at the web site below.

**http://www.efn.org/~rick/tour/**

3. Try turning your slogan into the front page of a travel brochure. Inside the brochure, be sure to include information about:

   - place's weather
   - where to stay
   - where to eat
   - sights to see
   - sports and other recreational activities

4. Use your spelling strategies to practise challenging words.

5. **Proofread** your brochure using the Read Aloud strategy on page 73.

Film reviewers describe a movie's plot and actors and rate movies — the more stars, the more they liked it. Would you see this movie?

**A Suspicious Town! \*\*\*\***

A mysterious stranger arrives in a small town. When he starts asking questions about the town's history, local folks become nervous. In a role that's a departure for him, Alex Costas, the stranger, is serious, quiet, and secretive. As he exposes old secrets, the stranger finds himself in a dangerous situation. Directed by Marjorie Lee and also starring Nadine Liebman, *A Suspicious Town* takes the audience on a delicious, suspenseful adventure. **(PG)**

What parts of speech were the words ending in **-ous**?

## WORD MENU

jealous

gracious

fabulous

humorous

ambitious

nervous

furious

enormous

mysterious

delicious

dangerous

serious

famous

curious

# Creating Your Word List

### Say these words:

Say the new word created when the **suffix -ous** is added to:

| humour | fury | fame | grace |

What sound does **-ous** make? It has the final unstressed syllable sound "əs." **Suffix -ous** means "having" or "full of."

1.   As a class, make a list of words that end in **-ous**. Record the words on a class chart.

2.   Create the list of **-ous** words you will be learning to spell. You can use: the Word Menu, the review, your own words. Add your Lesson Words to the chart.

3.   **In your notebook**
   • Write the Lesson Words and circle each **suffix**.
   • Add **-ous** words to your Personal Dictionary. Refer to it often to add interesting words to your writing.

## Create a Mnemonic Device

You can make up simple phrases to help you remember the spelling of words. For example: a fri**end** to the **end**, **fur**ious **fur**. These memory helpers are called **mnemonic devices**.

# Working with Words

1. **Strategy Practice**   Look through your Lesson Words. Try to create a **mnemonic device** for 5 of your Lesson Words. Share your device with a partner.

2. **Syllables**   Write all of your Lesson Words, using a coloured hyphen to break up the syllables. For example: e ▪ nor ▪ mous.

3. **Sorting Words**   Write each of your Lesson Words on small pieces of paper. Sort by meaning, sort by spelling pattern, sort by **vowel sound**. Can you think of other ways to sort your words?

4. **Meaning Match**   Find the pairs of synonyms in the box and write them in your notebook.

| | | |
|---|---|---|
| nervous | fabulous | tremendous |
| dangerous | enormous | hazardous |
| envious | wondrous | jealous |
| anxious | luscious | delicious |

**CHALLENGE**   Use 5 of these words in a sentence.

5. **Changing y to i**   Say the following words to a partner: **grace**, **ambition**, **fury**, and **mystery**. How does the pronunciation change when you add **-ous**?

6. **Making Posters**   Read the film review at the beginning of the lesson. Make a poster advertising the movie. Be sure to make it colourful and imaginative. Discuss your poster with a partner.

**QUICK TIP**

Remember: **e** softens **g** and **c**. You must keep the **e** in words like **courage** and **advantage** when adding **-ous** to maintain the correct pronunciation (courag**eous**, advantag**eous**).

**7. Writing Workshop** Authors and artists often have distinctive signatures. Do you know of anyone famous who has a unique signature? Develop your own unique signature.

**AT HOME**

**8. Film Review** Review a film you have seen on TV or at the theatre. Rate the movie from 1 to 4 stars. Share your review with the class. Would others want to see this movie based on your review?

**9. Word Web** Write the word **mysterious**. What 2 words does it make you think of? What other 2 words do you think of? Add as many words as you can to make a Word Web.

> **CHALLENGE** Use your Word Web to write a story or poem.

**10. Mystery Word** Print a Lesson Word on a card or in your notebook. Use a card to cover all the letters except the first. Have a partner guess the hidden word. Move the card to show one more letter at a time until your partner guesses the word.

**11. Sentence Completion** Complete these sentences:
   **a)** I feel nervous when …
   **b)** I am curious about …
   **c)** People should be gracious about …
   **d)** The most enormous creature I have
      seen is …

**12. Roots and Suffixes** Write the root word for each word in the first column. Then add another suffix to write a new word.

| Word | Root | New Word |
| --- | --- | --- |
| industrious | industry | **a)** |
| nutritious | **b)** | **c)** |
| suspicious | **d)** | **e)** |
| fictitious | **f)** | **g)** |

84

# Focus on Language  DESCRIPTIVE SYNONYMS

A **thesaurus** is a book of words, usually in alphabetical order. Beside each word is a list of **synonyms**. You can use a thesaurus to find interesting words and expressions. Some thesauruses also list a few **antonyms**.

Two very boring words that many people use in their writing are **pretty** and **nice**.

1.  Find more descriptive synonyms. Brainstorm some now.

2.  If you must use the word, use a **simile**. For example:

    as pretty as a porpoise     as nice as a friendly neighbour

    Write 3 of your own similes for each word.

3.  Look through your writing folder to find words that you overuse. Brainstorm a list of synonyms you can use to replace your overused words. Keep your list handy. When you are revising and editing your work, use the list to replace overused words.

4.  Find a piece of writing; it can be poetry, prose, or nonfiction. Choose four words and replace them with synonyms.

5.  Replace the following underlined words from the lesson opener with synonyms.

    A <u>mysterious</u> stranger arrives in a <u>small</u> town. When he starts <u>asking</u> questions about the town's <u>history</u>, local folks become <u>nervous</u>. In a role that's a departure for him, Alex Costas, the <u>stranger</u>, is <u>serious</u>, <u>quiet</u>, and <u>secretive</u>. As he <u>exposes</u> old secrets, the stranger finds himself in a <u>dangerous</u> situation. Directed by Marjorie Lee and also starring Nadine Liebman, *A Suspicious Town* takes the audience on a <u>delicious</u>, <u>suspenseful</u> adventure.

**FLASHBACK**

How can the introductions to each spelling lesson give you ideas for story writing?

Enjoy this North American Aboriginal poem:

### An Indian Hymn of Thanks to Mother Corn

See! The Mother Corn comes hither, making all
hearts glad!
Making all hearts glad!
Giving her thanks, she brings a blessing; now,
behold! she is here!

Yonder Mother Corn is coming, coming unto us!
Coming unto us!
Peace and plenty she is bringing; now behold!
she is here!

— *anonymous*

## WORD MENU

worrying
agreeing
freeze
freezing
paying
satisfy
satisfying
hurrying
diving
dividing
flying
hiking
shining
pleasing
leaving

## Creating Your Word List

**Say these words:**

• Say the new word created when **-ing** is added to:

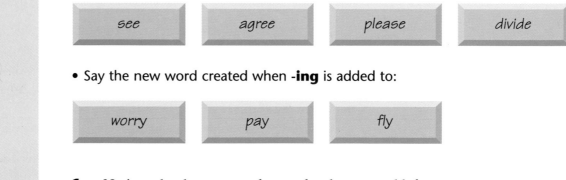

| | | | |
|---|---|---|---|
| *see* | *agree* | *please* | *divide* |

• Say the new word created when **-ing** is added to:

| | | |
|---|---|---|
| *worry* | *pay* | *fly* |

**1.** Notice what happens to the words when you add **-ing**:

> seeing, agreeing, pleasing, dividing, worrying, paying, flying

What changes were made to some of the root words?

**2.** Work with your teacher to create the list of **-e, -y + -ing** Lesson Words. You can use: the Word Menu, the poem, your own words.

### 3. In your notebook

- Write the Lesson Words and underline **-e**, **-y**, and **-ing**.
- Add challenging **-ing** words to your Personal Dictionary.

## Follow Suffix Rules

Here are rules that are generally true for adding suffixes:

- In words ending in a **long vowel + silent e**, drop the **e** when adding a suffix beginning with a vowel (pav**e** + **ing** = pav**ing**).
- If a word ends in **y** and the suffix doesn't begin with **i**, change **y** to **i** and add the suffix (ic**y** + **ness** = ic**iness**).

# Working with Words

**1. Word Recognition** Find the Word Menu word that has:

  **a)** 3 e's    **b)** **sat** inside    **c)** **row** backwards

**2. Spelling Rules** Find the Word Menu words or other words that follow these rules:

  **a)** Change **y** to **i** and add **-ed**.
  **b)** Change **y** to **i** and add **-es**.
  **c)** When 2 vowels go walking, the first does the talking and says its own name.
  **d)** Drop the **silent e** when adding **-ing** or **-ed**.

**3. Word Pole** Copy and complete this Word Pole. Use the clues to write Word Menu words. The letters in the pole will name an activity that's "for the birds."

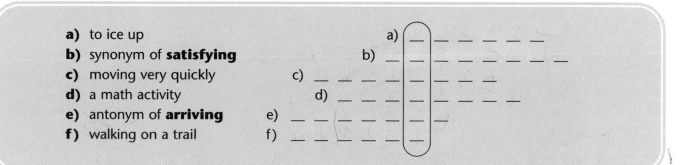

**a)** to ice up
**b)** synonym of **satisfying**
**c)** moving very quickly
**d)** a math activity
**e)** antonym of **arriving**
**f)** walking on a trail

4. **Writing Workshop**    When you are writing poetry, you can vary the number of words on each line. Look carefully at the poem on page 86. Why did the poet set up the poem this way? Rewrite the poem so that there is a complete sentence on each line. How do the meaning and rhythm change?

5. **Word Analogies**    Complete each analogy in your notebook:
   a) **sizzling** is to **hot** as _____ is to **cold**.
   b) **Driving** is to **car** as _____ is to **airplane**.
   c) **Honest** is to **dishonest** as _____ is to **disagree**.
   
   **CHALLENGE**    Write 2 more analogies to share.

6. **Adding -ing**    Read these words:
   a) hike    b) bike    c) poke
   d) dive    e) bake    f) shape

   What kind of vowels do you hear? Add **-ing** to each word and write the spelling rule the new word follows. Now read these words:
   g) hop    h) stop    i) step
   j) bat    k) run    l) wax

   What kind of vowels do you hear? Add **-ing** to each word and write the spelling rule the new word follows.

7. **Making Lists**    The poem at the beginning of the lesson describes what Mother Corn gives to the people. Make a list of things you would like Mother Corn to bring you. Illustrate your list and share it with a partner.

## QUICK TIP

Remember these rules for adding **-ing** and **-ed**: When a 1-syllable word ends in a short vowel/consonant pattern, double the final consonant (ste**p** – ste**pp**ed, ste**pp**ing). But do NOT double the final consonant in words that end in **x** (fi**x** – fi**x**ed, fi**x**ing).

## ● DID YOU KNOW ?

**Flies** (insects) and **flies** (what a bird does) are homographs. The word **homograph** comes from 2 ancient Greek words: *Homos* means "same," and *graphein* means "to write."

**AT HOME**

8. **Word Web**    What activities do you find **pleasing**? Which activities are **displeasing**? Use each word to begin a Word Web. Make each web as large as possible.

# Focus on Language  HOMOGRAPHS

Homographs are words that are spelled the same but have different meanings. Sometimes homographs have different pronunciations: **wind** (wind — a breeze) and **wind** (wīnd — to twist or turn around).

Usually homographs share the same pronunciation: **saw** (a tool) and **saw** (past tense of "to see").

**1.** Write in your notebook the homograph pairs that answer the riddles. Use words from the box. For example:

A sour pastry. A **tart tart**

    **a)** A quick hunger strike.
    **b)** Tease a child.
    **c)** Spotted a tool.
    **d)** A lamp that's not heavy.
    **e)** A factory that makes growing things.
    **f)** A parade in the third month.
    **g)** A so-so carnival.
    **h)** Spot the secret agent.

| | |
|---|---|
| saw | march |
| plant | fast |
| light | fair |
| spy | kid |

**2.** Choose any 2 homograph pairs above and use each pair in a sentence. Use your proofreading strategies to **proofread** your sentences.

**3.** Think of 3 homograph pairs that would make humorous illustrations. Try drawing them.

A ball ball    The top top    A batter batter

**FLASHBACK**

How can telling homograph jokes help you in your spelling?

Look for words that end in vowels in this menu:

## Pizza Italia Menu

Your choice of:

| Cheese | Vegetables | Meat | Spice |
|--------|-----------|------|-------|
| Romano | tomato | pepperoni | oregano |
| Mozzarella | zucchini | salami | basil |
| Gorgonzola | broccoli | bacon | thyme |
| Parmesan | mushrooms | prosciutto | hot pepper |

| Toppings | Small | Medium | Large |
|----------|-------|--------|-------|
| One | 6.00 | 8.50 | 10.25 |
| Two | 6.75 | 9.50 | 11.50 |
| Three | 7.50 | 10.50 | 12.75 |
| Additional | 0.75 | 1.00 | 1.25 |

Try our delicious panzerotti     3.50

**WORD MENU**

potato

area

pizza

zero

formula

ski

data

solo

piano

menu

video

volcano

camera

mosquito

echo

## Creating Your Word List

• **Say these words:**

> **zero, patio, potato**

What vowel ending do these words share? What sound does this ending make? It makes the sound of **long o**.

• **Say these words:**

> **area, data, camera**

Did you notice that the vowel ending makes the sound of **short a**?

• **Say these words:**

> **menu, flu, spaghetti, ski**

What sounds do the vowel endings make in these words? They make the sound of **long u** (men**u**) and **long e** (confett**i**).

1. Make a list of words that end in **a**, **i**, **u**, and **o**. As you read each word out loud, STRESS the sound of the **vowel ending**.

2. Work with your teacher to create the list of words that end with the pronounced vowels you will be learning. You can use: the Word Menu, the pizza menu, your own words.

3. **In your notebook**
   - Write the Lesson Words and highlight the **vowel endings**.
   - Add challenging words to your Personal Dictionary.
   - What language do many words that end in **i** come from?

# Working with Words

1. **Forming Plurals**   Use the Quick Tip to help you write the plural forms of these words. When in doubt, use a dictionary.
   **a)** zero   **b)** solo   **c)** patio   **d)** mosquito
   **e)** video   **f)** motto   **g)** tomato   **h)** volcano

   **CHALLENGE**   Can you write the plurals of these words? Which words already ARE plural? Check in a dictionary.
   **a)** data   **b)** formula   **c)** focus   **d)** ox   **e)** sheep

2. **Alphabetizing**   Write these words in alphabetical order horizontally on one line.

   | formula | prosciutto | tomato |
   | --- | --- | --- |
   | echo | potato | gorgonzola |

   Circle the small words you find between. For example:

   ar (**ea**    **r**)atio

## QUICK TIP

Here are tips for making **-o** words plural: If a vowel comes before **o**, add **-s** (studi**os**). If a consonant comes before **o**, add **-es** to most words (potat**oes**). If the noun is a musical term, just add **-s** (pian**os**).

**3. Menus**   Write your own menu using Lesson Words and other words you know. Use as many words that end in a vowel as you can. Create a class display of menus. Enjoy!

**AT HOME**

**4. Doodle!**   Doodle 3 words at home that you want to practise spelling.

**5. Word Meanings**   Write the **Across** and **Down** clues that go with each "artistic" word in this crossword puzzle.

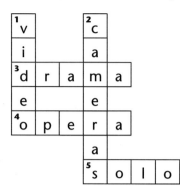

● *DID YOU KNOW?*

The word **piano** comes from the Italian word *pianoforte*. This is short for *clavicembalo con piano e forte* ("harpsichord with soft and loud").

**6. Irregular Plurals**   List the names of at least 5 animals whose last letter is a vowel. Add the plural form in a chart like this:

| Animal | Plural |
| --- | --- |
| gorilla | gorillas |

**7. Writing Workshop**   You can tell a story with the help of a video. If you have home videos, use them for story ideas.

**FLASHBACK**

Did you use the Come Back Later strategy? If so, did it help you write more quickly and easily? If not, try it!

## Advertising

Look at these examples of print advertisements for fast food. Advertisers want to sell you their product! Every day, you will see advertisements — on television, on billboards, on cars and trucks, in the paper, and in advertising fliers.

1. Watch for fast-food advertisements in newspapers, fliers, and magazines.

2. Pick 5 advertisements that you think are effective — they make you want to buy the food.

3. Look at the language these advertisements use (adjectives and adverbs, contractions, catchy phrases), the images they show, and special gimmicks (use of colour, close-ups).

4. Make a chart of your findings. You can set up your chart like this:

|   | Company | Language | Images | Gimmicks |
|---|---------|----------|--------|----------|
| 1 |         |          |        |          |
| 2 |         |          |        |          |
| 3 |         |          |        |          |

5. Decide on a product that you want to advertise. Based on your research, design an advertisement for a newspaper, magazine, or flier. Include words and images that will make people want to buy your product.

6. Check your spelling and layout before you make a final copy. Display your advertisement with those of your classmates.

# Spell·Check

**Patterns**
contractions
au, augh, aw
suffix -ous
-e, -y + -ing
vowel endings

**Strategies**
1. Identify words in a contraction.
2. Doodle your words!
3. Create a mnemonic device.
4. Follow suffix rules.
5. Come back later.

## Creating Your Word List

**In your notebook**
- Go to your list of "Words I Still Need to Practise."
- Pick 15 words you need to practise spelling. These are your Review Lesson Words.

## Working with Words

1. **Come Back Later**    Ask a partner to dictate your words. Leave a blank if you are not sure of a letter.

2. **Strategy Practice**    Doodle some of your words, and create a mnemonic (memory) device for other words.

3. **Bumblebee**    Play the Bumblebee game with a partner. Player A chooses a Lesson Word and writes down a dash for each letter of the word. Player B has to figure out the word by guessing 1 letter at a time. Only 1 guess of the whole word is allowed. For every incorrect guess, Player A draws another part of the Bumblebee. Then switch roles.

4. **Adding Vowels**    Write your words with only the consonants. For example: **t _ _ ght**.
Now go back and add the vowels.

5. **Real and Fake Definitions**    Look up 5 unusual words in the dictionary. Jot down 1 meaning for each and then make up 1 phony definition for each. Read the words and their 2 meanings to a partner. Ask him or her to guess the real meaning for each word.

6. **Word Meanings**    Write the **au**, **augh**, and **aw** words that have these meanings:
   a) clumsy
   b) antonym of **son**
   c) a sale with bidding
   d) writer
   e) to illustrate
   f) uncooked
   g) to clap
   h) spectators
   i) baby deer

**AT HOME**

**7. Practise Your Spelling Words**  Look back at the Strategy Spot on page 43. Use some of the ideas to study your Review Lesson Words at home.

**8. Word Explosion**  Choose 3 of these words and "explode" them by adding as many prefixes and suffixes as you can.
  a) complete      b) care      c) happy
  d) graph         e) able      f) use

**9. Contractions**  Write the contractions you can make with each group of words. Then use as many of the contractions as possible in a poem or paragraph.
  a) I would       b) I should not     c) I do not
  d) I am          e) I did            f) I will
  g) I cannot      h) I will not       i) I did not

**Proofreading Spotlight**

### Dictionary Skills

You can find words you can't spell in the dictionary if you remember some spelling rules. For example, if a word starts with the following sounds, which letters should you look up?
- "**f**" sound: Start with **f**, then look up **ph**.
- "**j**" sound: Start with **j**, then look up **g**.
- "**k**" sound: Start with **c**, then look up **k**.
- "**s**" sound: Start with **s**, then look up **c**.

Here are some more tips:
- Look up a root word, and then tack on the prefix or suffix when you write it.
- A dictionary has guide words to help you quickly find the page you need.

### FLASHBACK

Cross off your list the words you can now spell. Which spelling rules are you using? Which ones do you still need to review?

What **compound words** do these picture formulas make?

A **compound word** is 2 smaller words joined to form 1 word. The 2 small words **make the meaning** of the compound word.

**WORD MENU**

somewhere
lonesome
barefoot
classroom
clipboard
roommate
warehouse
hardware
software
whenever
wherever
keyboard

## Creating Your Word List

**1.** Say the **compound word** created by each of these word formulas:

grand + daughter = ?
some + where = ?
fish + hook = ?
where + ever = ?

**2.** As a class, make a list of compound words. As you read the words out loud, pay attention to the sound of each word that makes up the compound.

**3.** Work with your teacher to create the list of **compound words** you will be learning to spell. You can use: the Word Menu, the picture formulas, your own words.
Include these 3 **challenge words** in your Lesson Words:

**outside, already, although**

**4. In your notebook**
- Write each Lesson Word and circle each word that makes up the **compound word**.
- Keep adding **compound words**, **challenge words**, and other interesting or unusual words to your Personal Dictionary list.

## Make Word Waves (Syllables)

A great way to remember how to spell a word is to feel its rhythm. The best way to do this is to mark off each syllable by making "Word Waves." Each wave is a separate sound that you **hear**. For example:

on to          re mem ber

# Working with Words

1. **Noting Syllables**    Write out your Lesson Words, marking off the "Word Waves." What do many Lesson Words have in common?

2. **Sharing Compound Words**    Say each Lesson Word with a partner. Partner A says the first half of the word and Partner B says the second half of the word. Then both partners say the complete word together.

3. **Forming Compounds**    How many compound words can you make from these words? You may use each word more than once.

   **a)** out          **b)** some          **c)** ware          **d)** body

   **e)** ball          **f)** side          **g)** where          **h)** room

   **i)** house          **j)** day          **k)** any          **l)** every

   **m)** thing          **n)** time          **o)** play          **p)** no

4. **Homophones**    **Homophones** are words that sound the same but are spelled differently and have different meanings. Choose the correct homophone to complete each sentence in your notebook:

   **a)** We smelled a new _____ at the perfume counter. (**cent**, **scent**, **sent**)

   **b)** I loaded a new soft_____ program into my computer. (**ware**, **wear**, **where**)

   **c)** They bought jeans at the clothing _____house. (**ware**, **wear**, **where**)

   **d)** My dog follows me _____ever I go. (**ware**, **wear**, **where**)

   **e)** _____ my best friend. (**Your**, **You're**)

   **CHALLENGE**    Write 3 other homophone pairs or trios. Use one pair in a sentence. Continue adding homophones to your class list.

QUICK TIP

In compound words, all the letters of both joined words are present. There is a group of compound words in which a letter is lost. Compounds made with the word **all** drop one **l**: **al**most, **al**ready, **al**so, **al**though, **al**together.

**5. Writing Workshop**   Sometimes you can use pictures to help tell a story. This is what children's books do. Examine a children's book, focusing on the illustrations. Use illustrations to help tell the next story you write.

> ● *DID YOU KNOW ?*
>
> **Compound words** of 3 or more words are common in German. English evolved as a Germanic language, but has replaced many of its straightforward compounds with fancier words from other languages. There are only a few **triple compounds,** such as **insideout, upsidedown, whosoever, insofar, heretofore,** still found in English.

**6. Compound Completion**   Brainstorm 10 compound words. Play the Matchmaker game with a partner. Make a deck of 20 playing cards, writing one-half of a compound on each card. For example:

| foot | ball |
|------|------|

Shuffle and deal all of the cards. Player A places a card on the table with the word facing up. If Player B can attach a word card to complete a compound, she or he plays. If not, she or he passes. The first player to get rid of all of her/his cards wins.

**AT HOME**

**7. Finding Compounds**   There are many compound words hidden around your house. Make a list. For example: **bedpost**, **stairway**.

**8. Zookeeper**   Match up scrambled word parts to make compound words. Write the new words.

| bumble | ant |
|--------|--------|
| fly | snake |
| eater | butter |
| rattle | bee |

Ilustrate 3 of your compound words to show the 2 smaller words.

**CHALLENGE**   Make each of these into compound words by adding other words:
**a)** board      **b)** foot      **c)** some      **d)** ever

# Focus on Language  SENTENCE VARIETY

Use different types of sentences to give your stories variety:
- **statements:** Let's go to the concert.
- **questions:** Where would you like to sit?
- **exclamations:** The performance was fantastic!

Combine separate sentences that have related ideas into longer, smoother ones. There are lots of possible ways of combining.

Combine sentences with **co-ordinating conjunctions** (**and**, **but**, **or**, **for**, **yet**, **so**, **nor**).
- **separate:** The piano played. The tune was beautiful.
- **combined:** The piano played **and** the tune was beautiful.
- **separate:** Marie sang a solo. She was off-key.
- **combined:** Marie sang a solo, **but** she was off-key.

Combine sentences using **phrases**.
- **separate:** We responded to the drama. We cheered loudly.
- **combined:** **With a loud cheer**, we responded to the drama.
- **combined:** **Cheering loudly**, we responded to the drama.

**1.** Look at the menu on page 90. Write a statement, a question, and an exclamation about the menu. Label each sentence as a **statement**, **question**, or **exclamation**.

**2.** Combine each group of sentences using (**1**) a **co-ordinating conjunction** and (**2**) a **phrase**:
- **a)** The violinist played a solo. He played poorly.
- **b)** I ordered ravioli. I ordered in Italian.
- **c)** The audience applauded. Everyone stood up. They shouted "Bravo!"

**3.** Choose a paragraph you have written recently. Use sentence variety to make it more interesting and easier to read.

### FLASHBACK

Think about the compound words you studied in this lesson. Why are compound words easy to spell?

Like a film review, a book **synopsis** (brief outline) gives information about the plot and characters. Based on its synopsis, would you read this book?

Two girls from a small country town have received scholarships to study in London, England. Efra and Maria are best friends. They play the same instrument, share the same hobbies, and they both love adventure. Efra and Maria are also amateur crime solvers, and when an exciting case comes their way, they cannot turn it down. Their latest case proves to be more difficult than it appeared. The two land in trouble with the London police department, and their friendship is challenged in a way they did not think possible.

How many **suffixes** can you find in the synopsis? List them.

## WORD MENU

statement
friendship
apartment
department
entertainment
announcement
basement
relationship
movement
environment
ownership
instrument
experiment
hardship
treatment

## Creating Your Word List

**Say these words:**

- Say the new word created when the **suffix -ment** is added to:

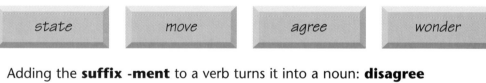

| state | move | agree | wonder |

Adding the **suffix -ment** to a verb turns it into a noun: **disagree** ("to quarrel") + **-ment** = disagreement (the result of a quarrel).

- Say the new word created when the **suffix -ship** is added to:

| hard | owner | relation | companion |

The **suffix -ship** forms words that mean "to be." Friendship is being a friend.

1. As a class, make a list of words that end in **-ment** and **-ship**. As you read the words out loud, STRESS the sound of **-ment** and **-ship**.

2. Work with your teacher to create the list of **-ment** and **-ship** words you will be learning to spell. You can use: the Word Menu, the book synopsis, your own words.

### 3. In your notebook

- Write each Lesson Word and <u>underline</u> the suffix.
- Add **-ment** and **-ship** words to your Personal Dictionary list. Keep it up to date to help in your writing.

**STRATEGY SPOT**

## Find Root Words

If you are not sure how to spell a word, look for a smaller root word inside it. Start by writing the root word.

# Working with Words

**1. Root Words**   Write the root word of 7 of your Lesson Words.

**2. Roots and Suffixes**   Write the root word for each word. Then add **-ment** or **-ship** to each and write the new words.

a) paying     b) based     c) exciting     d) stated
e) friendly   f) enjoying   g) judged      h) hardly

**CHALLENGE**   Write a brief definition of each **-ment** and **-ship** word you wrote.

**3. Adding Endings**   Copy this chart and use Lesson Words and other **-ment** words you know to complete it.

| root word | + ment | + other endings |
|-----------|--------|-----------------|
| pay | payment | pays, paying |

**QUICK TIP**

Adding **-ment** does not usually cause a spelling change. **Judgement** can also be spelled **judgment**.

**4. Rearranging Letters**   Rearrange and use all the letters in these words to make 2 other words. For example:

seam = mesa, same

a) read     b) loop     c) tame     d) rose
e) pins     f) lame     g) mean     h) snip

**5. Writing Workshop**   Reread the paragraph at the beginning of the lesson. Brainstorm a list of events that could happen in the story.

**6. Word Meanings**   Copy and complete this puzzle. Use the clues to write Word Menu words. Unscramble the letters in the circles to name an arranged meeting.

**a)** a motion

**b)** makes music

**c)** 2 or more things that are related

**d)** a type of sentence

**e)** ecology is concerned with this

**f)** the condition of possessing something

**g)** a news statement

**h)** done in science class

**i)** how you treat someone

**j)** a section of a store

a) _ _ _ _ _ _ _◯

b) ◯_ _ _ _ _ _ _ _

c) _ _ _ _ _ _ _◯ _ _ _

d) _ _◯_ _ _ _ _

e) _ _ _ _ _ _◯ _ _

f) ◯_ _ _ _ _ _

g) _◯_ _ _ _ _ _ _ _

h) _ _◯_ _ _ _◯_ _

i) ◯_◯_ _ _ _ _

j) _ _◯_ _ _ _ _ _ _

**AT HOME**

**7. Announcement**   Write an announcement about a specific event in your family. Share your announcement with a partner.

> ● *DID YOU KNOW ?*
>
> The word **monument** has no root word in English. The **suffix -ment** was added to the Latin verb *monere,* "to remind." A monument is a structure having "the means of reminding."

**8. Foldover**   Fold a piece of paper like a fan. Make 6 folds. Print a Lesson Word you want to practise on the first fold. Fold over so you can't see the word. On the next fold write the word again. Open up the paper and check your spelling. Repeat practising your word on each fold. Be sure to check for the correct spelling each time you write the word.

**FLASHBACK**

How can playing with words improve your vocabulary and spelling?

102

# *Literature*

## Shape Poetry

Shape poetry does not follow strict rules. When you write a shape poem, you do not have to worry about writing complete sentences or rhyming words. Here is an example of a shape poem.

## Ten Steps to Writing a Shape Poem

1.  Choose a noun that you can draw (some nouns, like **wind** and **air**, are difficult to draw).

2.  Think of your noun. How does it look, feel, taste, sound, smell? Brainstorm at least 15 words that describe it.

3.  Record the words on a piece of paper. Use your spelling strategies to help you spell the words.

4.  Check your spelling by looking up the words in a dictionary.

5.  Select 10 words from your list that you think best describe the noun.

6.  Draw an outline, in pencil, of your noun. When you are satisfied with its shape, trace it using a marker, paint, or crayon.

7.  Cut out your outline.

8.  Write the words in your outline. You can write them vertically (|), horizontally (–), and diagonally (/). You can also use different types of letters like bubble, capital, computer-made, squiggly, and block letters.

9.  Decorate your poem by highlighting some or all of the words.

10. Make up a catchy title and attach it to your poem. Now you're ready to share your poem with others.

**WORD MENU**

curler

regular

thirteen

popular

century

nuclear

solar

calendar

furniture

dirty

burning

temperature

urgent

irritate

separate

What **r**-controlled vowel sounds do you hear in this article?

### Halley's Comet

Mark July 28, 2061 on your calendar. That's when Halley's Comet makes its thirty-first appearance in our night sky. The comet's last visit occurred in February–March 1986, but it was barely visible to those of us who live in the Northern Hemisphere. The comet, which passes our Earth about every seventy-five years, was first recorded in China in 239 BC. Its head is a "dirty snowball" of frozen gases and cosmic dust that begin to thaw as the comet approaches the sun. They form the glowing coma that surrounds the nucleus of the head. As the comet nears the sun, the gases and dust are forced into an illuminated tail that can be 160 million km long. As Halley's Comet travels to the far end of our solar system, scientists continue to study its mysteries and marvels.

Did these letter patterns have similar sounds?

## Creating Your Word List

**Say these words:**

| arrival | thirteen | irritate | curler |
|---------|----------|----------|--------|

How similar are the sounds made by **ar**, **ir**, and **ur**? Does their position in a word (beginning, middle, end) affect pronunciation?

**1.** Make a list of words that contain **ar**, **ir**, and **ur**. As you say each word out loud, STRESS the sound of **ar**, **ir**, and **ur**. Organize the words in a chart like this:

| ar | ir | ur |
|----|----|----|
|    |    |    |

2. Work with your teacher to create the list of **ar**, **ir**, and **ur** words you will be learning to spell. You can use: the Word Menu, the article, your own words. Add your Lesson Words to the chart.

3. **In your notebook**
   - Write each Lesson Word and circle **ar**, **ir**, and **ur**.
   - Practise difficult words by using them in your writing.
   - Add **ar**, **ir**, and **ur** words to your Personal Dictionary.

**STRATEGY SPOT**

## Spell a Word by Sound and Sight

Here are 3 tips for spelling a word that contains **ar**, **ir**, or **ur**.

1. Pronounce each word carefully — you may hear a slight difference in the pronunciation of each pattern (f**ar**, f**ir**, f**ur**).

2. Think about which spelling looks right (sh**ir**t or sh**ur**t?).

3. Create a visual image or mnemonic device (d**ir**ty b**ir**d).

# Working with Words

1. **Missing Letters**   Add **ar**, **ir**, or **ur** to complete each word in your notebook. Hint: 3 words can be completed using more than 1 letter combination.
   a) f _ _ ther
   b) g _ _ age
   c) rad _ _
   d) e _ _ ly
   e) regul _ _
   f) st _ _
   g) b _ _ ning
   h) he _ _
   i) c _ _ ry
   j) bl _ _
   k) ch _ _ p
   l) _ _ gent

2. **Illustrating Phrases**   Draw a picture for each phrase. Label each picture and underline the shared letter pattern.
   a) shark army
   b) dirty shirt
   c) turning Saturn

   **CHALLENGE**   Make up at least 2 phrases you can use to practise spelling challenging words. Share with the class.

3. **Recognizing Patterns**   Write the word in each group that does NOT belong.
   a) thirteen, thirsty, whirling, thrifty, thirty
   b) regular, popular, collector, particular, cellar
   c) burning, turning, squirming, churning, hurling

**QUICK TIP**

To remember that calen**dar** ends in **ar**, think of Jan**uar**y and Febr**uar**y — the first 2 months of the calendar.

**AT HOME**

**4. Graphing**   Ask someone at home to help you record names of household items that contain **ar**, **ir**, and **ur**. Count the number of words with each pattern and prepare a graph of your findings.

**5. Rearranging Letters**   Drop and rearrange letters to make new words:

| nuclear |
|---|
| **a)** drop 2 letters to find a relative |
| **b)** drop another to get a hint |

| regular |
|---|
| **c)** drop 2 letters to get a size |
| **d)** drop another to get anger |

| century |
|---|
| **e)** drop 2 letters to get a cease-fire |
| **f)** drop another to find a remedy |

| burning |
|---|
| **g)** drop 2 letters to take something along |

**6. Writing Workshop**   Reread the paragraph at the beginning of this lesson. It is one example of nonfiction writing. Here are other examples of nonfiction forms of writing:

- autobiographies
- biographies
- book reviews
- descriptions
- dictionary entries
- editorials
- instructions
- letters
- narratives
- newspaper articles
- pamphlets
- photo captions
- recipes
- reports
- reviews
- timelines

Choose a topic and write about it using 1 of the above forms, or some other form of nonfiction writing. Write your first draft. Check that the information makes sense, and then ask a friend to edit your draft. Include all changes in your second draft. Finally, proofread for spelling and grammar errors. Display your finished nonfiction writing so that others may read it.

**FLASHBACK**

How would you help a friend who has trouble spelling **ar**, **ir**, and **ur** words?

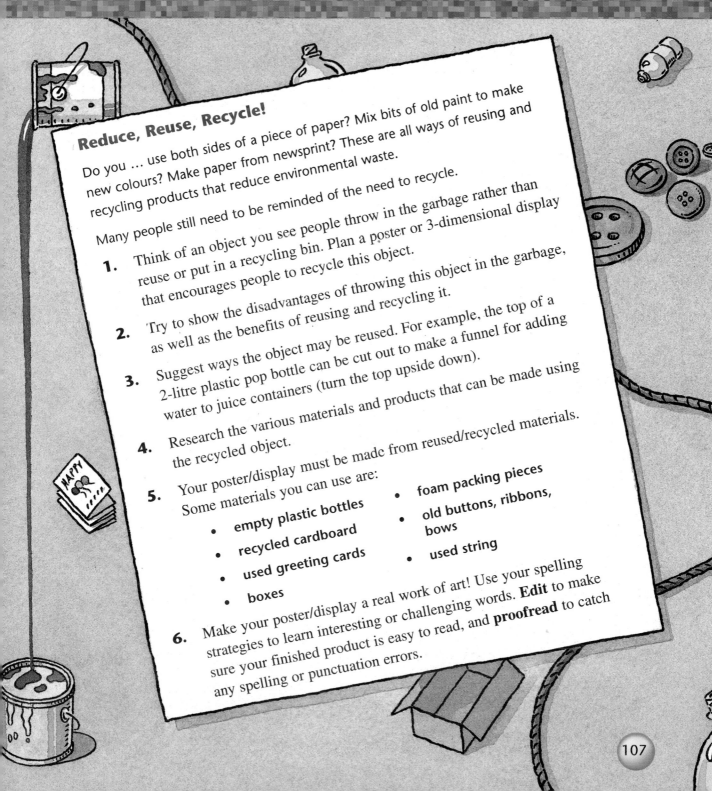

## Reduce, Reuse, Recycle!

Do you ... use both sides of a piece of paper? Mix bits of old paint to make new colours? Make paper from newsprint? These are all ways of reusing and recycling products that reduce environmental waste.

Many people still need to be reminded of the need to recycle.

1. Think of an object you see people throw in the garbage rather than reuse or put in a recycling bin. Plan a poster or 3-dimensional display that encourages people to recycle this object.

2. Try to show the disadvantages of throwing this object in the garbage, as well as the benefits of reusing and recycling it.

3. Suggest ways the object may be reused. For example, the top of a 2-litre plastic pop bottle can be cut out to make a funnel for adding water to juice containers (turn the top upside down).

4. Research the various materials and products that can be made using the recycled object.

5. Your poster/display must be made from reused/recycled materials. Some materials you can use are:

   - **empty plastic bottles**
   - **recycled cardboard**
   - **used greeting cards**
   - **boxes**
   - **foam packing pieces**
   - **old buttons, ribbons, bows**
   - **used string**

6. Make your poster/display a real work of art! Use your spelling strategies to learn interesting or challenging words. **Edit** to make sure your finished product is easy to read, and **proofread** to catch any spelling or punctuation errors.

See how adding a **prefix** changes the meaning of these words.

comfort — **dis**comfort

complete — **in**complete

measurable — **im**measurable

## WORD MENU

dishonest

disagree

disappeared

impossible

impatient

disgrace

disconnect

imperfect

disobey

invisible

insecure

inactive

dislike

discourage

## Creating Your Word List

**Say these words:**

- Say the new word created when the **prefix dis-** is added to:

### able, comfort, honest

The **prefix dis-** can mean "not" (**dis**honest — not honest) or "opposite of" (**dis**connect — do the opposite of connecting).

- Say the new word created when the **prefix in-** is added to:

### complete, active, visible

- Say the new word created when the **prefix im-** is added to:

### possible, patient, polite

The **prefixes in-** and **im-** can mean "not" (**in**visible — not visible, **im**polite — not polite).

1. Make a list of words that use these prefixes. Put them into a chart like this:

| dis- | in- | im- |
| --- | --- | --- |
|  |  |  |

**2.** Work with your teacher to create the list of **dis-**, **in-**, and **im-** Lesson Words you will be learning to spell. You can use: the Word Menu, the illustrated words, your own words.

**3. In your notebook**
- Write the Lesson Words and highlight the **prefixes**.
- Add **dis-**, **in-**, and **im-** words to your Personal Dictionary list. Keep it up to date to help in your reading and writing.

**STRATEGY SPOT**

## Make a Missing Letter Puzzle

Doing a Missing Letter Puzzle like the one below can help you learn to spell a word. The blank spaces focus on parts of the word you need to study.

# Working with Words

**1. Missing Letters**   Fill in the missing letters in your notebook to write Word Menu words.

**a)** _ i _ a _ _ ear   **b)** d _ _ o _ e _   **c)** _ _ pat _ _ nt
**d)** im _ _ _ fect   **e)** _ _ _ h _ _ _ st   **f)** _ _ p _ ss _ _ _ _
**g)** _ _ _ cour _ _ e   **h)** _ na _ _ i _ e   **i)** _ _ _ agr _ _

**CHALLENGE**   Make a Missing Letter Puzzle on the computer.

**2. Removing Letters**   Start with the word **impatient**. Follow the directions and write the new words.
  **a)** Remove 2 letters to find "someone who is in the hospital."
  **b)** Remove 2 more letters to find "liquid colour."
  **c)** Remove 1 more letter to find "an ache."
  **d)** Remove 1 more letter to find a cooking container.
  **e)** Remove 1 more letter to find a two-letter **article**.

Now start with **impolite**. Make the letters disappear to discover new words. How many new words can you make?

**3. Word Explosion**   "Explode" the words below by adding **prefixes** and **suffixes**. Write as many new words as you can. Use a dictionary to check each word.
**a)** agree   **b)** appear   **c)** honest   **d)** like

impatient

**QUICK TIP**

The **prefixes il-, im-,** and **ir-** are all variations of **in-**. Before **l**, use **il-**. Before **r**, use **ir-**. Before **b**, **m**, or **p**, use **im-**.

**4.** **Prefix Hunt**   Look through the newspaper to find words with the prefixes **dis-**, **im-**, **in-**. Copy out 3 sentences with these prefixes.

**5.** **Noting Syllables**   Slowly say each Lesson Word and quietly snap, clap, or tap out the syllables. Write each word, using coloured hyphens (-) to separate the syllables.

**6.** **Antonyms**   Write an **antonym** (opposite) that begins with **dis-**, **in-**, or **im-** for each of these words:

| | | | | | | | |
|---|---|---|---|---|---|---|---|
| **a)** | visible | **b)** | secure | **c)** | patient | **d)** | agree |
| **e)** | regard | **f)** | possible | **g)** | please | **h)** | jointed |
| **i)** | active | **j)** | partial | **k)** | appear | **l)** | connect |

CHALLENGE   Most of the time **dis-** and **im-** mean "not." But they can have other meanings. Add the prefixes **dis-** and **im-** to **prove**. What happens? Which prefix gives the word its opposite meaning?

---

● *DID YOU KNOW ?*

The **prefix pre-** means "before" or "in front of." The word **prefix** comes from a Latin word meaning "to place in front."

---

**7.** **Concentration**   Cut a sheet of paper into 20 equal-sized squares. Write your Lesson Words twice — 1 word per square. Turn the squares over, and mix them up. Number the **back** of the squares from 1 to 20. Take turns turning over 2 numbers until you get a pair of matching words.

**8.** **Writing Workshop**   Sometimes using the word **not** is more effective than using a prefix. It stresses your point and can be written in capital letters for emphasis. For example: I am NOT pleased. Look through your writing folder. Are there any places you should use **not** instead of a prefix?

FLASHBACK

How does knowing the meanings of prefixes and suffixes help your vocabulary grow?

## Taking Notes

Learning how to take good notes is an important skill. You will take notes all your life — in school, at home, and at work. Taking notes helps you to remember facts that you have read or heard. Good notes include key words and phrases (the most important words and phrases). To practise making notes, begin by reading these paragraphs about Inuit carvers.

## The Image Carvers
### by Barbara Brundege and Eugene Fisher

The Inuit hunters of Cape Dorset, Northwest Territories, turn stone into stunning art. First they get soapstone from quarries; then with their skilled hands they carve lasting images of their lives on the land.

Soapstone is used for the carvings. To get it, carvers journey to the soapstone quarries of Korak Inlet. They pitch tents on the bluffs above the quarries. The soapstone is found in rock veins within the earth. Lifting the heavy stone from the quarry is hard work.

Many carvers are or have been hunters, with a special knowledge of the animals of the North. They are keen observers, and they capture what they see in their soapstone carvings.

1.  With a partner, take turns describing the main topics of the text. Jot down these topics.

2.  On your own, make notes of the material. Work with one paragraph at a time. Read each sentence and record key words and phrases.

3.  You can use short forms of words (NWT — Northwest Territories) to make your notes shorter. Use your own words to describe an idea ("To get it, carvers journey to the soapstone quarries of Korak Inlet" — Carvers travel to Korak Inlet to get stone).

4.  If you find it helpful, draw a picture to help you remember other facts in the text.

5.  Reread your notes to check that they make sense.

6.  With your partner, compare your notes. Did you record the same information? If no, discuss reasons for the differences.

Read this script dialogue:

> Mulder *(examining artifacts at an exhibition of Inca art)* : Look, this ancient inscription shows an extraterrestrial astronaut sitting at a spaceship control panel!
>
> Scully: Relax, Mulder. We're on vacation, not on a mission. It's simply an Inca priest.
>
> Mulder: Well, that may be the official story. But I think there's more to it. Just be patient while I ask the curator a few questions.

Which words in the dialogue had the sound of **"sh"**? What letter patterns made this sound?

**WORD MENU**

action
patient
official
invention
exhibition
mission
tension
issue
nation
ancient
social
shall
shout
special
mansion

## Creating Your Word List

- **Say these words:**

  **shall, shout, spaceship**

  What sound does the letter pattern **sh** make?

- **Say these words:**

  **ancient, special, suspicion**

  What sound does the letter pattern **ci** make?

- **Now say these words:**

  **action, exhibition, mission, tension**

  The patterns **ti**, **ss**, and **si** in these words also make the **"sh"** sound.

1. As a class, make a list of words that contain the **"sh"** sound. Put the words into a chart like this:

| "sh" words | | | | |
|---|---|---|---|---|
| sh | ti | ci | si | ss |
|  |  |  |  |  |

2. Create the list of **sh**, **ti**, **ci**, **si**, and **ss** words you will be learning to spell. You can use: the Word Menu, the dialogue, your own words. Add your Lesson Words to the chart.

3. **In your notebook**
   • Write each Lesson Word and <u>underline</u> the letter patterns that make the **"sh"** sound.
   • Keep adding new **"sh"** words to your Personal Dictionary.

**STRATEGY SPOT**

## Remember the Order of Letters

Some letters tend to be in certain places in a word. For example, **ci**, **ti**, **si** tend not to be at the end of a word. Try to remember what letters do not complete words.

# Working with Words

1. **Circling Patterns**   Write out your Lesson Words and circle the spelling patterns using different colours:
   • red for middle patterns
   • blue for ending patterns
   • green for beginning patterns
   Did you notice anything about the patterns?

2. **Pattern Recognition**   Pick the correct spelling in each row. Then use 3 of the words in interesting sentences.

   | | | | |
   |---|---|---|---|
   | **a)** | speciel | spesial | special |
   | **b)** | tention | tension | tenssion |
   | **c)** | mantion | mancion | mansion |
   | **d)** | mention | mentian | mension |

**QUICK TIP**

The **"sh"** sound can also be spelled these ways: **ce** (o*ce*an), **s** (*s*ure), **ch** (ma*ch*ine), **sci** (con*sci*ous).

3. **Synonyms**   Try to write at least 1 **synonym** (similar meaning) for each Lesson Word. Use a thesaurus or dictionary if you need help.

4. **Antonyms**   Write the Lesson Words that mean the opposite of:
   **a)** anxious   **b)** whisper   **c)** informal   **d)** ordinary

   **CHALLENGE**   Write a definition for each word you wrote, using your own words.

**5. Concentration**   Cut a sheet of paper into 20 equal-sized squares. Write your Lesson Words twice — 1 word per square. Turn the squares over, and then mix them up. Number the **back** of the squares from 1 to 20. Lay the squares down so that the numbers are showing. Take turns turning over 2 numbers until you get a pair of matching words.

**6. Word Meanings**   Play "I'm Thinking of a Lesson Word" with a partner. Pick a Lesson Word. Give your partner a clue about it. See if your partner can guess the word in 3 tries.

**7. Word Formulas**   Complete these formulas to write the new words.

a) invention – ion + ed =        b) exhibition – ion + ing =

c) patient – t + ce =        d) specialist – ist + ize =

e) nation + al + ity =        f) ownership – ship – er + dis =

**CHALLENGE**   "Explode" each word you made by adding and subtracting endings and prefixes. Check your new words.

● **DID YOU KNOW ?**

When the pattern **ch** has the **"sh"** sound, it usually is in a word that comes from French (**ch**andelier, **ch**auvinist, **Ch**arlotte).

**AT HOME**

**8. Strategy Practice**   Use your spelling strategies to practise 4 tricky words in your Personal Dictionary list.

**9. Word Web**   Pick 1 of your Lesson Words. What 2 words does it make you think of? What other words does each new word make you think of? Add as many words as you can to make a Word Web.

**CHALLENGE**   Use your web as the basis for a story or poem you write in class or at home.

**10. Writing Workshop**   How is a script different from dialogue that uses quotation marks? Look back at the dialogue on page 112. Use what you know about punctuating dialogue to rewrite the conversation using quotation marks. See page 15 for information on using quotation marks and other punctuation. You may want to use dialogue in your next story.

# Focus on Language  COMMAS

Here are some rules for punctuating your writing using commas:

- Use a comma to separate the items (words, phrases, numbers) in a list or series.

  The Six Nations Confederacy includes the Cayuga, Mohawk, Oneida, Onondaga, Seneca, and Tuscarora.
  Friday, October 31, 2012

- Use a comma after such introductory words as **No** and **Well**.

  Well, let's visit the Six Nations Art Gallery.

- Use a comma to set off words of address.

  Shania, look at that beautiful painting of a bear.
  Are you taking notes for our group project, Taso?
  Dear Lee,

- Use a comma before a conjunction (examples: **and**, **but**, **or**) that joins two complete sentences.

  Our group gave a talk about our visit to the Six Nations Art Gallery, and the other students said they'd like to visit it too.

1.  Copy and punctuate these sentences, adding necessary commas.
    a) My favourite subjects are math art and social studies.
    b) I biked across the street over the bridge and into the park.
    c) Yes my sweater is an official NHL product.
    d) On Saturday March 25 1950 my dad was born.
    e) I threw a party to celebrate the new year but most of my friends already had made other plans.

2.  Read a paragraph in one of your textbooks. Note how commas are used. Can you find examples of the 4 uses of commas?

### FLASHBACK

How can you help yourself remember the various ways to spell the **"sh"** sound? Share your ideas with a classmate.

# Spell · Check

**Patterns**

compound words
suffixes -ment, -ship
ar, ir, ur
prefixes dis-, in-, im-
"sh" sound

**Strategies**

1. Make Word Waves (syllables).
2. Find root words.
3. Spell a word by sound and sight.
4. Make a Missing Letter Puzzle.
5. Remember the order of letters.

## Creating Your Word List

**In your notebook**

• Go to your list of "Words I Still Need to Practise."
• Pick 15 words you need to practise spelling. These are your Review Lesson Words.

## Working with Words

1. **Make Word Waves**   Write out your Review Lesson Words, breaking them into syllables by using Word Waves.

2. **Finding Root Words**   See how many of your words contain root words. Write each root word, and then write the Review Lesson Word you found it in.

3. **Mnemonic Devices**   Create visual images or mnemonic devices to help you remember the spelling of 3 of your words.

4. **Compounds**   Are any of your Review Lesson Words compounds? Write the smaller words that make up each compound word.

5. **Adding Consonants**   Write your words with only the vowels. For example: _ **o** _ **ia** _
   Now go back and add the consonants: social.

6. **Word Meanings**   Write the **"sh"** sound words that have these meanings:
   a) yell       b) calm         c) a deed, movement
   d) carnival   e) special job, task   f) subject, topic
   g) country    h) large home   i) old

   CHALLENGE   Use the words you wrote or other **"sh"** words in a crossword puzzle. Trade with a partner.

AT HOME

7. **Practise Your Spelling Words**   Look back at the Strategy Spot on page 43. Use some of the ideas to study your Review Lesson Words at home.

**8. Choosing Synonyms** Rewrite this passage, replacing the **bold** words with synonyms from the box below.

> We moved our **tools and machinery** to the site and began to dig for remains of a **very old** civilization. If we found an artifact our **understanding** would be **moved forward**. The earth gave way to **reveal** an **underground** staircase. We counted **a dozen + one** steps as we peered into the **darkness**. As I **began** to **use a ladder** down I was filled with a sense of **terror**, as if some unknown **force** was waiting for me at the bottom.

| | | | |
|---|---|---|---|
| buried | thirteen | started | equipment |
| ancient | climb | power | shadows |
| advanced | horror | show | knowledge |

**CHALLENGE** Complete the story using your own ideas.

Proofreading Spotlight

## Use a Thesaurus

A thesaurus can help you replace dull, tired, overworked words in your writing. Look up these words in your thesaurus and write 2 synonyms for each word.

**a)** gloom    **b)** nervous    **c)** seat    **d)** trap    **e)** travel

Said is one of the most overused words. Brainstorm all the ways you can say something. Think of different situations. Add to your list by looking up each new word in a thesaurus. Keep this list of synonyms handy in your writing folder!

*Look at one of your stories that contains a lot of dialogue. Replace some of the* **saids** *with more interesting synonyms.*

### FLASHBACK

Set a spelling goal for next year.

Find the silent-consonant items in this picture.

calf

halves

climber

doubtful

resign

signpost

knuckle

knob

knit

autumn

column

wrinkle

wrist

written

## Creating Your Word List

**Say these words:**

signpost    knob    column    wrinkle

These words share one characteristic — they each contain a **silent consonant**. Say each word again and notice the letter that is not pronounced.

**1.** As a class, make a list of words that have **silent consonants**. Record your words in a chart like this:

| Silent consonant - beginning - | Silent consonant - middle - | Silent consonant - end - |
|---|---|---|
|  |  |  |

**2.** Work with your teacher to create the list of silent consonant Lesson Words you will be learning to spell. You can use: the Word Menu, the picture, the dictionary, your own words.

### 3. In your notebook
- Write the Lesson Words. Circle the silent consonants.
- Add silent consonant words to your Personal Dictionary list as you meet them in your reading. Keep your dictionary up to date to help in your reading and writing.

## Helpful Hints

There are several activities that help you to spell words that contain silent consonants. Here are two suggestions.

### Visualize Words

Write down the Lesson Word. Cover the word and imagine that you still see it. Try to picture the word in your mind. Can you spell the word using your mental picture to help you? Uncover the word and check to see that you spelled it correctly.

### Imaginary Writing

If you have difficulty spelling a word, write it with your finger — in the air, on your desk, in your notebook. Spell it softly. Does your "writing" feel right? If yes, write the word in pencil or pen. If no, repeat the activity before checking a dictionary.

# Working with Words

1. **Sorting Silent Consonants**   Sort your lesson words by their silent consonants.

| l | b | gn | kn | mn | wr |
|---|---|----|----|----|----|
|   |   |    |    |    |    |

    a) What type of letter comes after a silent **l**?
    b) What letter often comes before a silent **b**?
    c) What silent letters are followed by **n**?
    d) What letter often comes after a silent **w**?

2. **Silent Letter Words at Home**   Make a list of 15–20 items in one room of your home. Circle all the silent letters in these words.

3. **Word Puzzles**   Make up puzzles that use words containing silent consonants. Two types of puzzles you can make are crossword puzzles and word-search puzzles. If you make a crossword puzzle, use words that are familiar to both you and whoever will be completing the puzzle. (Using little-known words can make a crossword puzzle very difficult to complete.) If you make a word-search puzzle, you don't have to worry about including difficult words because you supply a word list. A dictionary can be a great source of new words to use when you make this kind of puzzle.

4. **Writing Workshop**   Sharing your written work (poems, stories, nonfiction) is an important part of being an author. With whom can you share your work? What kinds of comments can you make when someone shares his or her work with **you**?

5. **Silent-Consonant Art**   Make a collage of silent-consonant words. You can make your collage eye-catching by writing words in a variety of ways (painting, string, glitter), and by creating and cutting out pictures of silent-consonant words.

6. **Word Stairs**   Write down a Lesson Word or other silent-consonant word. Ask a partner to use the last letter of the word to begin a new word. Take turns to see how long you can make your flight of stairs.

```
c l i m b e r
            e
            w
            r
            i
            t
        e i g h t
```

● **DID YOU KNOW?**
In 1455 Johannes Gutenberg invented a new way of printing using movable type. Before that time few books were written and many people did not know how to read (or spell). With this invention, standardized spelling — spelling words the same way — began to be important.

# Focus on Language  ▶ VISUALIZATION IN WRITING

In this lesson, you have seen how visualization can help you spell words. You can also use visualization to help you write creatively, especially when beginning to write a story.

Do you ever get a great idea for a story but when you sit down and turn on the computer or pick up a pen, nothing happens? You write a few sentences, and then immediately erase what you have written. This is not how you imagined your story would be.

Here is a simple visualization exercise that will help. If you like, you can record the exercise in your notebook.

**1.** Sit in a comfortable position and close your eyes.

**2.** Draw your character in your mind. What does she or he look like?

**3.** What is your character's personality — happy? sad? worried? carefree?

**4.** Ask your character "Who are you?" and "What is happening to you?"

**5.** Look for details that surround your character. Are there other people in the picture, or is your character in a setting that you could write about?

**6.** When you are finished (there is nothing more to see and your "drawing" begins to disappear) open your eyes.

**7.** Pick up your pen or return to your keyboard.

**8.** Start writing using your mental images!

You can use visualization to help you at all stages of draft writing.

**FLASHBACK**

How have you grown as a speller? What are 5 strategies or patterns you have learned?

Notice all the things the dictionary tells us about prefixes and suffixes.

> **prefix** (prē′ fiks) *n.* letters added at the beginning of a word to change its meaning: *When you put the prefix "dis" in front of the word "appear," you get "disappear." pl.* **prefixes**.

> **suffix** (su′ fiks) *n.* letters added at the end of a word to change its meaning: *When you add "ance" to the end of the word "appear," you get "appearance." pl.* **suffixes**.

## WORD MENU

reappeared

impossible

careless

watchful

precaution

recycle

interactive

intelligence

unthinkable

irregular

subscription

wondrous

leadership

## Creating Your Word List

• **Say these words:**

  **recycle, interactive, irregular**

What sounds do the **prefixes re-**, **inter-**, and **ir-** make?

• **Say these words:**

  **careless, wondrous, intelligence**

What sounds do the **suffixes -less**, **-ous**, and **-ence** make?

**1.** Make a chart with these headings:

| Prefixes | Suffixes | Prefixes and Suffixes |
|---|---|---|
|  |  |  |

List each Lesson Word under one of these heads. For words that contain both a prefix and a suffix, list them under the third heading.

**2.** Work with your teacher to create the list of Lesson Words you will be learning to spell. You can use: the Word Menu, the dictionary entries, your own words.

**3.** Add other words that contain prefixes and/or suffixes to your Personal Dictionary. Keep it handy when you read and write.

STRATEGY SPOT

## Spelling Rules

Suffixes can cause spelling problems. To help you, think of spelling rules that you know. For example, you drop **e** when you add the suffixes **-er** and **-ed** — **examine** becomes **examiner** and **examined**.

# Working with Words

**1.** **Selecting Words**   Complete each sentence by selecting one of the following words. Write the complete sentence in your notebook.

| interview | flexible | telephone |
| --- | --- | --- |
| educational | professional | superintendent |

**a)** Petra found her trip to the Inca ruins very _____ .

**b)** Amber is a _____ engineer.

**c)** The _____ rang throughout the day.

**d)** The building _____ looked with dismay at the damaged floor.

**e)** Laura dreaded the two-hour _____ .

**f)** Jan needed a _____ work schedule so he could be home by 4:00 P.M. each day.

**CHALLENGE**   List other words that contain prefixes and suffixes and write sentences like these. Can a partner complete your sentences?

**2.** **Writing Workshop**   You can tell a story using audiotape or videotape. How are these forms of story different from written stories? What special skills would you need to tell audio and video stories?

**3. Exploding Words** Look at how the word **use** can be "exploded":

disuse reuse misuse use user useful usage

Explode these words by writing as many new words as you can. Check in a dictionary to ensure that your new words make sense.

**a)** print   **b)** port   **c)** able   **d)** clear

**● DID YOU KNOW ?**

The prefix **inter** comes from Latin and can mean three things: "together" (**interweave**), "between" (**interrupt**), and "between or among groups" (**interclass**).

**QUICK TIP**

Remember, in words that end in **y**, change it to an **i** before adding a suffix.

**4. Word Definitions** You will need 12 pieces of paper for this activity. Select 6 words that contain a prefix or a suffix and write them on separate pieces of paper. On the remaining 6 pieces of paper, write definitions for the words. Place the slips of paper face down on a table. Ask a partner to flip the papers and match the words with their definitions.

**CHALLENGE** Repeat the activity several times, each time using new words and definitions. Ask your partner to time you. When finished, find your average sorting time and your personal best time.

**AT HOME**

**5. Prefixes and Suffixes in Print** Look at print materials at home — newspapers, magazines, advertising flyers, books. Go on a prefix and suffix hunt to find 10 new words. Use 2 or more of these words in a message to a member of your family.

**FLASHBACK**

Review strategies you have learned to help you spell words that contain prefixes and suffixes. What strategies have you used the most?

## Completing Patterns

In English, letters and sounds often follow patterns that repeat in predictable ways. Math is like a language because it also has predictable patterns. In this lesson, you completed sentences by filling in missing words. In this activity, you will complete patterns using shapes instead of words.

1. Copy the pattern on a piece of paper. Use a pencil so that you can try different answers and erase those that don't work. When you have finished, write out the sequence the pattern follows. For example, it might be: **square, square, circle, triangle, triangle.**

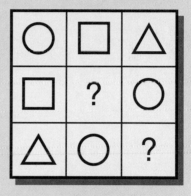

2. Ready for something more challenging? Solve these 2 patterns.
   **a)** What is the sequence?             **b)** What is happening here?

3. **CHALLENGE**   Make your own pattern puzzle for others to solve. Write the sequence that you have used on a piece of paper and fold it so the answer does not show. Leave your puzzle and the answer where classmates can work on their own to solve it.

Spelling **S T R E T C H**

Find out more about words and make your spelling skills stretch in this special section of exciting games and extra challenges. Your teacher will show you which activities are just for YOU.

## 1. Jobs!

**a)** In your notebook, match the jobs listed in the box with the clues below.

**b)** Record the first letter from each job, in order from **1** to **8**, to discover the goal of every job hunter.

**c)** Rank your interest in each job (1 – very interested; 8 – have no interest).

| | | | |
|---|---|---|---|
| architect | interpreter | dentist | illustrator |
| roofer | musician | electrician | hypnotist |

**1.** I can draw my way out of a situation.
**2.** I can help you to build on your ideas.
**3.** I am instrumental in putting my point across.
**4.** You will do exactly as I say.
**5.** I can help you to say that in another language.
**6.** You might say my job always takes me to the top.
**7.** I try not to let anything shock me in my job.
**8.** I'm always filling in for someone.

## 2. Laughing Words

**a)** Complete these sentences in your notebook by choosing a "laughing" word that goes best with the sentence meaning. Use each word only once.

| | | |
|---|---|---|
| chuckle | roar | giggle |

Allan began to _____ when he realized what had happened.

I let out a _____ when I saw the clown get a pie in the face!

Although it wasn't very funny, Jill did manage a small _____ when she heard the pun.

**b)** Write sentences in your notebook using these laughing words.

| | | |
|---|---|---|
| snicker | crow | howl |
| guffaw | chortle | cackle |

3. **Edit the Politician**   Ana Novotem, the politician, uses too many words in her speeches. Rewrite the following speech in your notebook, deleting unnecessary words and phrases. You can also change or add words and punctuation to make the meaning clearer.

> "Welcome, hello, greetings, ladies and gentlemen, friends, guests, to my usual Wednesday morning talk on the issues of the day. I have good, incredible news that I want to share with all of you now, and I will tell it to you, each and every one of you. Our new library, which will have many books and reading material and tapes and CDs and computers and people working in it, will be built and constructed right here, in this place, on this spot where we are sitting in just one year's time, only twelve months! I'm sure that you are just as thrilled, excited, happy, overwhelmed as I am, and that you will be delighted and enthusiastic to know that the building will be made. Thank you, all of you, thank you, again and again."

4. **Fantabulous!**   What do you get when you combine the names **Europe + Asia**? What do you get when you combine the words **smoke + fog**?

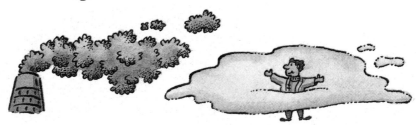

continued on the next page ...

These words are examples of **portmanteaus** – new words that have been made by combining parts of 2 existing words. Here are some other portmanteaus.

motor      + hotel  = motel
melt       + weld   = meld
breakfast + lunch  = brunch

**a)** Make portmanteaus using these word combinations. Write your new words in your notebook.

splash + surge =            rise + shine =
spot + blotch =             table + chairs =
vegetable + hamburger =     soap + water =
mean + stingy =             jump + shout =
broiled + roasted =         dogs + cats =

**b)** Make up more portmanteaus using words of your choice. Give them to a friend to see if he or she can guess the 2 words that make up each portmanteau.

**c)** Use some of your portmanteaus from **a)** and **b)** in a story or a poem you are writing. You can include illustrations of some of your portmanteaus.

5. **Shortening Words**   Some words can be shortened and still keep their original meaning. For example, **gymnasium** can be shortened to **gym** and **chimpanzee** can be shortened to **chimp**.

**a)** Write the shortened version of these words in your notebook.

telephone        pantaloons       taxicab
milkshake        champion         veterinarian
examination      goodbye          submarine

**b)** Here are shortened versions of 10 words. Write the original (long) version of each of these words in your notebook. Use a dictionary if you need help.

deli    limo    flu    hippo    lab
gas     ump     bus    sax      plane

**c)** Many words that are new to our language refer to technology. Like other words, they may be shortened at some future time. For example, **computer** may become **comp** or **puter**. What technology words do you think will be shortened? In your notebook, write the words in full and then write how you think they will be shortened.

## 6. Picture This

a) Draw a word. Show something about its meaning in the way that you draw it. Here are three examples.

Draw these words and decorate them using coloured markers, pens, paper, or found materials.

| | | | |
|---|---|---|---|
| heavy | squeeze | quick | crazy |
| shout | flat | shrink | glide |

b) Draw these word pairs. Be as creative as you can!

| | |
|---|---|
| bread and butter | rough and ready |
| slip and slide | huff and puff |
| now or never | safe and sound |

## 7. Musical Words

Musical words are words that are spelled using only the letters in the musical alphabet: a, b, c, d, e, f, g. For example, **bag** is a musical word because **b**, **a**, and **g** are all part of the musical alphabet. **And** is not a musical word. Although **a** and **d** are in the musical alphabet, **n** is not.

Write as many musical words as you can in your notebook. For an extra challenge, see how many words you can make in a set period of time (for example, 5 min, 10 min).

## 8. Word Partners

a) Word partners are 2 or more words that go together. Two examples of word partners are **dogs and cats**, and **fish and chips**. Complete these 2-word partners using the words in the box. Write them in your notebook.

| day | found | clear | puff | dry |
|---|---|---|---|---|
| seek | water | shut | socks | pains |

huff and _____      lost and _____

hide and _____      wash and _____

open and _____      shoes and _____

night and _____      aches and _____

soap and _____      loud and _____

continued on the next page ...

**b)** Complete these 3-word partners using the words in the box. Write them in your notebook.

| jump | mineral | milk | lettuce | nose | away |
|---|---|---|---|---|---|

coffee, tea, or _____        bacon, _____, and tomato
up, up, and _____            ear, _____, and throat
hop, skip, and _____         animal, vegetable, or _____

**c)** Change some of the word partners from **a)** and **b)** to make new meanings, for example, *huff* and *puff* to *huff* and **bluff.** Record your new word partners, which can be funny or serious, in your notebook.

**9. Word Chains**   Word chains are created by linking words together like this:

- Select a "theme" word, for example, television.
- Use the last letter in the theme word to start a new word. The new word must relate to the theme word.
- Continue until no other words can be linked.

televisio(n      n)ew(s      s)how

**a)** In your notebook, create word chains for these theme words.

circus    supermarket    movies

**b)** Decide on a theme word and give it to a friend to use as the base of a word chain. For an extra challenge, time your friend.

**c)** A word fence uses other letters in your theme word as starting points. For example:

```
t e l e v i s i o n
e       i  y      e
l       d  n      w
e       e  d   s h o w
p       o  i
l          c
a          a
y          t
           i
           o
           n
```

**10. Crazy Phrases** A crazy phrase is a type of riddle. For example:

Since the word **man** appears over the word **board**, you get the phrase **man overboard**.

   **a)** What do these crazy phrases say? Write your answers in your notebook.

| | | | |
|---|---|---|---|
| **1** | somewhere<br>———————<br>the rainbow | **2** | head<br>———————<br>heels |
| **3** | ham<br>———————<br>rye | **4** | water<br>———————<br>swimming |
| **5** | weather<br>———————<br>feeling | **6** | on<br>———————<br>world |

**7**   e  a  p
    e     p
    s     p
     u a l

**8**   ɘʞɒɔ

   **b)** Create a crazy phrase and give it to a friend to solve.

**11. Similes** Similes compare 2 objects using the words **like** or **as**. For example:

       The *balloon* was **as** big as a *house*.
         The *kite* flew **like** an *eagle*.

   **a)** Use your own words to complete these similes and finish the sentence.

The ship sailed like a    _____ .
Our car was like a        _____ .
The baby was as quiet as a  _____ .
This work is like an       _____ .
She hit the ball like an    _____ .
He was as happy as an     _____ .

   **b)** Make comical similes that you can use in your writing. For example: heavy as a marshmallow, fast as a tortoise, and ran like a snail.

continued on the next page ...

**c)** Select 1 of your similes and illustrate it, using the simile as the title of your drawing. As an extra challenge, illustrate your simile but do not include the title. Can a friend guess the simile?

**12. Designing an Identity Card**  Create your own identity card. It should include the following information:
- your name
- a short, catchy phrase about you (a slogan)
- a logo or design

You might want to include other information. To help you decide what you will include, draw a rough draft on paper. Revise your draft until you are satisfied with it, then make a good copy on a piece of poster board. Your card can be any size, from wallet-size to poster-size, and can be any shape — rectangular, round, square, and so on. Post your completed card with those of your classmates. As a large group, decide on the most eye-catching card.

**13. Slogans and Business Cards**  Companies or businesses often have slogans or catchy sayings that make a positive statement about them. For example, a slogan for a restaurant might be "Meals at GREAT Deals!"

**a)** Match the company names in the box with the slogans listed below. Record them in your notebook.

| | | |
|---|---|---|
| Buzz Electric | Tiretown | Cheap Books |
| Shoppers' Galaxy | Bankland | Town Taxi |
| T.A.P. Plumbing | Pet Palace | |

Your money is our business
Comfortable, convenient, clean
Where reading is free (almost)!
Star bargains galore!
Our low prices are shocking!
Our prices are wheely low!
We'll treat them like royalty!
Make your troubles go down the drain

**b)** Create catchy slogans for these businesses.

Dial-a-Deli        Arctic Airlines
Fran's Cartown     Working Appliances

**c)** Make up a company. Decide on its name, the service it will provide, and a slogan that will catch customers' attention. Create a business card for your company that includes all important details.

**14. The ABC's of ...**

    **a)** How long would it take you to write a word for every letter of the alphabet? Give yourself a time limit of 5 minutes. To make the task easier, ask a partner to watch the clock for you so that you can devote your attention to writing. At the end of the 5-minute period, count how many words you were able to write.

    **b)** Make an organized alphabet word list based on a theme. For example, if you choose "entertainment," all the words you write, in order from A to Z, will relate to entertainment (for example, **actor**, **backstage**, **theatre**).

    **c)** Select one of the following themes.

| | | | |
|---|---|---|---|
| food | technology | jobs | sports |
| music | countries | names | animals |

Make an alphabet word list using your selected theme. If you're not sure of a word, check it in your dictionary.

**CHALLENGE**   For an extra challenge, organize teams, select a theme, and start writing. See which team can make the most words in a set amount of time.

**15. Ancient Stems**   Many of our words are built on Latin and Greek word stems. For example, **aqua**, **cent**, and **octo** are Latin word stems while **astro**, **graph**, and **sphere** are Greek word stems.

    **a)** Match each of the 6 stems above with these meanings and record them in your notebook.

| | | |
|---|---|---|
| something written | stars | eight |
| a ball, globe | hundred | water |

    **b)** Match these word stems with their meanings and record them in your notebook.

| | | | |
|---|---|---|---|
| auto | mono | mem | micro |
| zoo | flex | ped | ject |

| | | | |
|---|---|---|---|
| single, one | animal | self | throw |
| keep in mind | small | bend | foot |

continued on the next page ...   133

**c)** Select any 5 word stems from **a)** and **b)**. Write as many words as you can think of on your own for each stem. For example: **aqua**: **aquarium**, **aquanaut**, **aquatic**, **Aquarius**. When you run out of ideas, use a dictionary to help you find other words that share the stem.

**16.** **Sports Language**   Baseball language has many abbreviations. Here are two examples: **AB** means "at bat," **HR** means "home run."

    **a)** Match the abbreviations in the box with the baseball terms below.

| LOB | RBI | B | E | OF |
|-----|-----|-----|-----|-----|
| BA | SB | IP | ERA | HB |
| SO | SHO | 2B | WP | TP |

| | | |
|---|---|---|
| error | batting average | innings pitched |
| outfield | left on base | shut-out |
| runs batted in | winning pitcher | stolen base |
| earned run average | bunt | hit batter |
| triple play | double | strikeout |

    **b)** Hockey also uses some abbreviations. For example, **GA** means "goals against." List other hockey abbreviations that you know in your notebook. Look in the sports pages of a newspaper for ideas.

    **c)** Create some hockey abbreviations for these terms.

| | | |
|---|---|---|
| blue line | forecheck | boarding |
| penalty minutes | back-check | breakaway |
| pure hat trick | offside | drop pass |
| pull the goalie | face-off | poke check |
| cross-check | high stick | |

    **d)** Write a short report of a baseball or hockey game using abbreviations instead of full words. Ask someone who is not familiar with the sport to read your report. Can she or he understand the report, or do they need help? What does this tell you about the use of abbreviations?

**17.** **Names that Tell**   People tend to categorize insects as bugs, but they're much more than that! For example, a **fly** could be a *firefly*, *a greenbottle fly*, a *scorpion fly*, or even a *big green darner dragonfly*! These names tell more about the insect than the word **fly**.

a) What kinds of **beetles** are there? There's an *engraver* beetle, a *soldier* beetle, even a *whirligig* beetle. Write down the names of other types of beetles. Use a dictionary or science resource to help you.

b) How many types of **butterflies** can you name? Make a list in your notebook. Remember to use a dictionary or other form of resource material to help you.

c) Imagine that you discover a new insect while exploring in the Rocky Mountains. Name and draw the insect; then tell something about its habits in a short report to be given to scientists.

18. **Borrowed Words**   Many of our words have been borrowed from other languages. To find out more about some of these words, match the clues below with the Borrowed Words in the box. Record each word and its clue in your notebook.

| Borrowed Words | | | | |
|---|---|---|---|---|
| gum | polo | coleslaw | ketchup | cinnamon |
| ill | tycoon | balcony | chipmunk | hamburger |

comes from the Italian *balco*, meaning scaffold

the Old Norse word, *illr*, gives us this word that means not well

an Old French word that originally came from Egypt, and describes something you chew

a game played on horseback; name comes from the Tibetan word *pulu*, meaning ball

a Native word that describes a small, squirrel-like animal

you may enjoy eating this, but its origin is the name of a city in Germany

the name of this red sauce comes from the Chinese *ke-tsiap*, meaning brine of pickled fish

this word is used to describe a powerful person and comes from the Japanese *taikun*, meaning mighty lord

a spice name that comes from the Hebrew *quinnamon*

the Dutch word, *kool sla*, for cabbage salad, gives us the name of this dish

19. **Terrific Tongue Twisters**   Tongue twisters are fun to read. They're even more fun to say — the faster the better! How fast can you say these 2 without twisting your tongue?

> She sells seashells by the seashore.
> Peter Piper picked a peck of pickled peppers.

a) Try these terrific twisters! Say each one out loud, and try to increase your speed without tripping over your twisting tongue.

Silly Sally spilled soup on Susie's suit.
Katie can catch but Cathy can't.
Frightened Freddie fainted frequently on Friday.
Lela Ladder lugged little lemons lightly.

b) Complete these twisters with your own words. Try to make them challenging but not so difficult that they are impossible to say.

Karl Kessler kept ketchup ...
Yolanda Yoman yodelled ...
Clifford Cleaver clumsily closed ...
Happy hippos like ...
Ziggy and Zinney zoomed ...
Shelley Sherman shivered ...
Spilled spaghetti ...
Wally wanted ...

20. **Compound Words**

a) In your notebook, combine the 10 single-syllable words on the left with those on the right to make 10 two-syllable compound words.

| | |
|---|---|
| car | boy |
| but | don |
| tea | pet |
| don | few |
| cow | pot |
| cur | tan |
| rat | get |
| for | ton |
| ham | key |
| par | let |

**b) Someday**, **somebody**, and **somewhere** are *some* examples of compound words that begin with the word **some**. How many others can you think of? Write them in your notebook, using a dictionary for help if you need it.

**21. Make a List**

a) What are some of your favourite people and things? Record the following headings in your notebook. For each, add as many entries as you can.

| My Favourite... |
| --- |
| Actors |
| Colours |
| Television Programs |
| Foods |
| Books |
| Musicians and Singers |

b) Make these lists in your notebook.
- names of all classmates
- a list of friends' birthdays
- countries where your classmates were born or have visited
- classmates' favourite lunches
- contents of your desk
- snacks you like
- birthday gifts you would like to receive
- everything you would take for a 2-year trip to Mars

Hint: You might want to keep a personal Book of Lists, which you can add to throughout the year.

**22. Clichés** Have you ever heard someone say that something was **easy as pie**? Maybe someone else was **going around in circles**. These expressions are called clichés. They are "tired" phrases that are often used in place of other words that have the same meaning. For example, easy as pie means very easy; going around in circles means that someone is lost or confused.

a) Match these meanings with the clichés on the next page. Write your answers in your notebook.

continued on the next page ...

| | | |
|---|---|---|
| reveal a secret | in danger | trick |
| say what you mean | stop | very bad |

grind to a halt                 pull the wool over one's eyes
rotten to the core             don't beat about the bush
hanging by a thread         let the cat out of the bag

**b)** What do you think these clichés mean? Write your answers in your notebook.

tear your hair out             a month of Sundays
with flying colours            not worth a plugged nickel
can't have your cake         go against the grain
  and eat it too

**c)** Rewrite these sentences. Replace the clichés (printed in **bold**) with regular words.

He's going to **pass the buck** on this one.
That's not my **cup of tea**.
I'm **all thumbs** when it comes to repairs.
She's the **spitting image** of Joan.
The coat just **vanished into thin air**.
After winning the race, Jeanette was **on cloud nine**.

**23. Descriptive Sentences**   Which of these statements is more descriptive?

She wept a lot.        She wept buckets of tears.

The second statement is more descriptive, but it's also an exaggeration. It's impossible to weep buckets of tears, but this phrase creates a strong image. When exaggeration is used to describe something, it is called **hyperbole**. Sentences that use hyperbole can make writing more interesting, as long as the technique is not used too much.

**a)** Use hyperbole to make these sentences more descriptive. Write the new sentences in your notebook.

He ran fast.
She answered many questions.
The rocket flew high.
That crocodile is old.
I can read lots of words quickly.

**b)** Tone down the hyperbole in these sentences. Rewrite them in your notebook using less exaggerated descriptions.

The dog searched for ages for its family.

We skied millions of times down that hill without getting hurt.

My uncle caught thousands of fish in his river last week, and each one looked bigger than my dad's car!

I searched through tons of newspapers looking for the article.

**c)** Select 1 sentence from your revised sentences for **a)**, or from the original sentences for **b)**. Draw a picture of the sentence that shows its exaggeration.

24. **Within Words**

**a)** How many smaller words can you find in **hippopotamus**? There's *hip, pot, must, tam, spot, pots,* and *math.* How many other words can you find? Write them in your notebook.

**b)** Try this challenge. Write down as many words as you can find in **Saskatchewan**. Ask a partner to time you (for example, 5 min).

**c)** With a partner or as part of a small or large group, write down as many words as you can find in **concentration**.

CHALLENGE Find words in **valentine, telephone, hospital, September, danger,** and **Manitoba**.

**d)** Select your own word, such as your name. List the smaller words you can make from the same letters.

25. **One = Twice the Riddle** Here's a riddle game where 1 word is related to 2 other words. In each case, the riddle word may relate to one or both words because it is a synonym, homonym, or antonym, or it may rhyme with 1 word and share another relationship with the second word. For example, you are given two words — **thunder** (rhyme) and **beneath** (synonym). You know that the riddle word must rhyme with thunder and have the same meaning as beneath. Your riddle word: **under**.

**a)** Discover the riddle words for these clues. Write the words in your notebook.

continued on the next page ...

food (synonym), squeal (rhyme)
to (homonym), shoe (rhyme)
fight (rhyme), day (antonym)
choose (rhyme), win (antonym)
in (antonym), shout (rhyme)
see (synonym), book (rhyme)
dwelling (synonym), mouse (rhyme)
car (rhyme), near (antonym)
short (antonym), wall (rhyme)
toad (rhyme), street (synonym)

**b)** Make up some of your own 2-word riddles. Give them to a friend to solve.

**26.  Homonyms**

**a)** Complete Josie's order list. In your notebook, write a homonym for each word printed in **bold**.

*Josie's Everything Shop*

a _____ to be on **sale** at 50% off

two **pairs** of _____ for the lunch table

one _____ with **links** to the zoo

a box of _____to remain **stationary** on the shelf

one _____ for the **night** shift

a tub of _____ flown in from **Greece**

some _____ shoots for the **seeder** out back

_____ buckets of fudge that I **ate**

one microscope slide of a muscle _____ that I can **sell**

the _____ who **bore** down on my car last week

_____ cartons of golf balls **for** my aunt

a _____ that lets me paint my cat's **claws**

one new **gnu** that I _____ in Africa

a _____ who **toed** the line when we _____ his home

10 **patients** who have the _____ to wait in line

**b)** Draw the interior of Josie's Everything Shop after all the orders have arrived and she has put everything in its place.

**27.  Anagram Wordplay**   Liven up your day with some anagram wordplay! An anagram is a word that has had its letters rearranged to make a new word. For example, **stop** – **pots** and **wed** – **dew** are anagrams. When making an anagram, you must use all of the letters in the original word.

Spelling **STRETCH**

**a)** Make anagram pairs by changing these words into new words. Write your anagrams in your notebook.

| who | aches | art | grin | ear |
|-----|-------|-----|------|-----|
| spit | left | live | part | read |

**b)** Complete these sentences by writing an anagram for each word printed in boldface.

I **won** my ___ trophy.
That **chase** gave me lots of _____ !
**Dear** Mary: Please ____ my letter.
**Could** that _____ rain on us?
I have to buy that _____ at **night**.
Dear **Diary**: Tomorrow I'll go to the _____ for milk.
The word **wolves** has two _____ .
He got some **bread** crumbs stuck in his _____ .

**c)** Discover some other anagrams. You might want to work with a partner or in a group. Exchange your anagrams with classmates to see if they can make new words.

**28.** **Collective Nouns**   We often think of **flock** and **herd** as typical names for groups of animals. However, did you know that *foxes* form a **skulk** and that *owls* get together in a **parliament**? Collective nouns for animals are anything but typical.

**a)** Match the collective names for animals using the clues provided below. Record the answers in your notebook.

| **Collective Nouns – Animal Groups** | | | | |
|------|------|--------|------|--------|
| gang | cast | plague | knot | string |
| pride | troop | siege | host | crash |

lions (proud)
locusts (sickness)
toads (to tie)
elks (group of people)
monkeys (a military group)
rhinoceroses (the sound of a jar hitting a hard surface)
ponies (use to tie things)
herons (a great battle)
sparrows (he or she greets you at a party)
hawks (actors in a play)

continued on the next page ...

**b)** Select 1 of the collective nouns from (a) and create a humorous illustration. With your classmates, create an Animal Groups bulletin board to display your work.

### 29. Sports Writing

**a)** Sportscasters and writers often use colourful language when describing events at a game. For example, if the Wings beat the Rockets, a sportscaster might report it as: "The Wings clobbered the Rockets!" What other ways might the Wings beat the Rockets? Write your answers in your notebook.

**b)** As sportswriter for *The Daily Blabber*, you must create great sports headlines. Write headlines based on the following game results. Make them as catchy as possible.

*Hockey Scores*
Montreal Canadiens: 6        New York Islanders: 0

*Baseball Scores*
Toronto Blue Jays: 12        Baltimore Orioles: 3

*Basketball Scores*
Vancouver Grizzlies: 112     Phoenix Suns: 84

**c)** Rewrite sports headlines that you have read in your local newspaper. Try to make them more descriptive by including colourful, interesting words.

### 30. Be a Banker

**a)** Imagine that you are a banker and need a dictionary just for you. What words would be important to a banker? They might be words like **loan**, **currency**, **accounts**, **interest**, and **security**. Write at least 10 other words that a banker might like to find in a banker's dictionary.

**b)** List your banker's words in alphabetical order and beside each word write its definition. Indicate which part of speech each word is (**noun**, **verb**, **adjective**, **adverb**).

**c)** Make a dictionary for 1 of the following occupations or use a job of your own choice. Make a list of at least 10 words that would be in the dictionary for that occupation. Put the words in alphabetical order and beside each write its meaning. Indicate which part of speech each word is.
- author
- farmer
- construction worker
- doctor
- teacher
- artist

# Word List

Words printed in **bold** are **challenge words**.